MW01027033

PUTTING

JESUS

FIRST

PUTTING

JESUS

FIRST

A 21-DAY
DEVOTIONAL JOURNEY
through **COLOSSIANS**

COURTNEY TRACY

B&H
PUBLISHING
BRENTWOOD, TENNESSEE

978-1-0877-5243-3

Published by B&H Publishing Group
Brentwood, Tennessee

Dewey Decimal Classification: 248.84
Subject Heading: BIBLE. COLOSSIANS--STUDY AND
TEACHING \ CHRISTIAN LIFE \ JESUS CHRIST

Cover design by Studio Nth, LLC.
Cover images by Chinnapong/shutterstock and Jenny_nature/
shutterstock. Author photo by Gretchen Hinz.

1 2 3 4 5 6 • 27 26 25 24 23

To Dakota—who knows me best and points me to the surpassing worth of Christ every day in the unseen moments, reminding me always to keep putting Jesus first. I love you, and for countless reasons, I could not have completed this devotional book without you.

To Collins, Thomas, and Charlee—who have kept on teaching me about the sufficiency of Christ and depending on Him and His strength in all things instead of my own. Mommy loves you! Daddy loves you! Jesus loves you most of all!

To my editor, Ashley—thank you for faithfully keeping Jesus first, highest, and best and pointing me to His supremacy as you've come alongside me to write the words that are within these pages for His glory.

To my pastor, Ben—thank you for always faithfully preaching the good news of Jesus according to His Word and for reminding me to keep putting Jesus first as this little devotional book was coming together. I am so grateful for the way you shepherd your flock and point us to the Good Shepherd who is before all things and sustains all things!

CONTENTS

INTRODUCTION

Hi, friend! As you are opening up the pages of this devotional study, can I just say, *I'm so glad you're here.* Life can be, and often is, so demanding. I'm not sure what season of life you may be in right now, but I *am* sure that whatever it is, there truly is no shortage of people, places, jobs, and the like that demand our attention each and every day. Whatever God has in front of you at the moment, I totally understand how much intentionality it takes to carve out some time to spend in God's Word. As a wife and mother with three children five and under, I know how difficult this can be! But I also know the immense joy and unrivaled fruit it produces in the life of the believer when we do choose to carve out time to meet with God each day in His Word and in prayer.

I don't know your current age or life-stage. Perhaps you're like me—a busy mom. Maybe you're a high school student or in college—spending your days studying, going to classes, working, participating in sports, and of course, enjoying your social life. Or, maybe you're a working professional, trying to pull off that ever-elusive balance between work life and personal life. You might even be a woman with older kids, darting between school drop-offs and activities, or maybe your season of life looks like doting on and helping with those busy grandkids.

Regardless of what life looks like for you, we all live in a world full of distractions, responsibilities, and noise. So friend, one of my prayers for this devotional book is that it would help give you a daily, habitual practice of meeting with God both in His Word and in prayer—and that this practice will encourage you to press on to maturity in Christ. As we journey through the book of Colossians together over the next twenty-one days, we will see some major themes that are not only applicable to the original audience of the book but are just as applicable to us today. I can't wait to get started with you!

———

How exactly will we journey through Colossians together? you may be wondering. Great question!

I've set this devotional book up for you so that you are given two days each week to catch up if you miss a day, or to save those days to reflect or explore further the parts of Colossians we have covered that week. In other words, this monthlong, twenty-one-day devotional guide allows you to read five new devotionals a week with two "rest" days over the weekend (or whenever fits your schedule best) with one extra day at the end to wrap up. My hope in structuring your experience this way is that it will give you some flexibility (life happens!) if you get behind a day and makes room for other Bible reading or studying (I pray!) you're doing outside of this little devotional book.

Each day we'll walk through a few things. First, you'll **READ** a new passage in Colossians; then you'll **REFLECT** with me as we glean powerful principles that God wants us not only to learn but also to live out. After reflecting on the passage, you'll find some questions I've provided to help you process and **RESPOND** to the passage on a personal level, so that the truths you've learned might make their way into your heart, mind, soul, and life! Each day you'll notice some new questions are featured. But here's a heads-up: each day will *also* include a few repeated questions you may see here or there. And that's on purpose! Those questions are:

1. What does today's passage teach me about God's character? (In other words, what you learned about God from today's passage!)
2. What hope does Jesus offer these Colossians and us today?
3. How can you live in response to this truth today? Because God is _____, I will _____.

Wait, why are we repeating these questions? Another great question. For two reasons. First, focusing on God's character reminds us that the Bible is a book about God. Every verse and passage we read in our Bibles tells us about *Him*. We can find His character on display in all of the Bible! To help you answer this question with specificity, I've included **a list of God's attributes and characteristics** in this devotional guide (*attributes* is just a fancy word for God's character traits). You'll find that list in the back of the book on page 176. Please use this resource as you reflect on His character each day. Think of it like a word bank to help jog your thoughts and learn more about God! I have loved and used a resource like this myself many times in my own reading and studying of God's

Word, so I pray this will be a blessing and help you as we walk through Colossians over the next several weeks!

Second, these repeated questions are offered not only to help you understand God's character on a *head* level but to connect on the *heart* level too—and more than that, to move out all the way into your *actions* in daily life (you'll notice that the third question noted above is meant to help you take what you've learned about God and exemplify or honor the attribute you identified about God). My prayer for you as we journey through Colossians together is not just that you learn some truths about God but that these truths will transform your heart and mind and that you respond to God's truth by living them out in your everyday life. That you will make a practice every day, in every circumstance, of putting Jesus first in your life above everything else.

To close each day, I've provided a **PRAYER** that will help you thank God for all He's teaching you, and as a bonus, you'll also find an **EXPLORE MORE** section added onto each day, just in case you happen to resonate strongly with a certain theme and want to learn more about it in the Bible. No pressure on that section—it's not as if you didn't finish your devotional reading for the day if you don't explore that whole section. It's just there to help you dive deeper if you prefer or have the extra time. Perhaps you can come back to these "explore more" questions on a day that there is no new devotional reading, or maybe even return to them the next time you pick up this devotional guide to walk through Colossians again.

On top of that, I've tucked away some **dive deeper tips** in the back of the book on page 177 for your convenience. If you find yourself curious about certain things you read, these study tips will give you the tools you need to help clarify things, dive deeper into the passages you're reading, and ultimately get the most out of the book of Colossians as we explore it together.

Ultimately, my heart for this devotional book is that you see the beauty and matchless worth of Jesus in a world that beckons us to bow our knees to other, lesser gods of our time (then and now!) and put Jesus where He belongs in your life: above all things. Whether you use this as a supplement to your time spent in God's Word or a launching pad into your Bible reading and studying of God's Word, (maybe you've always been intimidated to study the Bible—I know this feeling; so perhaps this devotional guide will turn out to be the thing that helps you take a step closer to doing that!), I hope this journey through Colossians gives you a place to develop a daily rhythm of meeting with God. I also hope the extras in this book offer you helpful Bible reading and studying tips that you can take with you in this lifelong, daily practice of meeting with God in His Word and in prayer so that, over the long haul, your days meeting with God will add up to a *whole life* shaped by the glory, beauty, and riches of the gospel of Jesus Christ.

So, now that you're prepared for what's ahead in the journey, I'll wrap up today's introduction with a few questions for you to consider before we embark on our journey through this wonderful book of the Bible, and I'll also offer two prayers. One is a prayer I am praying for you, right from the book of Colossians itself. The second is a prayer you can pray to the Father to prepare your heart for this journey. I can't wait to read and reflect deeply on the surpassing worth of Christ and the implications this has on every other part of our lives as we study Colossians together, friend.

RESPOND

1 / What are you looking forward to most about this devotional guide? What is one attainable goal you can set for yourself as we explore Colossians together?

2 / What is your greatest hope for this journey through Colossians? Your greatest fear, if any?

3 / Have you ever read through the whole book of Colossians before? Why or why not?

4 / Think through your life and schedule over the next twenty-one days. Of all the things ahead of you, what is most likely to distract you from this journey through Colossians? How can you anticipate these distractions and make a plan to overcome them?

5 / If you could pray one thing over this twenty-one-day journey, what would it be? Take some time to ask God for this right now. (And if you need some help finding the words, use the prayer below!)

COURTNEY'S PRAYER FOR YOU

Heavenly Father, I pray for this sister picking up this devotional guide through Colossians. I pray, God, that she may be filled with the knowledge of Your will in all spiritual wisdom and understanding, so as to walk in a manner worthy of You, fully pleasing to You: bearing fruit in every good work and increasing in the knowledge of who You are . . . (Col. 1:9–10). I pray that her heart may be encouraged, being knit together in love, to reach all the riches of full assurance of understanding and the knowledge of Your great gospel mystery, which is Christ . . . (Col. 2:2). And Father, I pray that as she has received Christ Jesus the Lord, Your Son, she would so "walk in him, rooted and built up in him and established in the faith, just as [she] was taught, abounding in thanksgiving" (Col. 2:6–7).

A PRAYER FOR YOU TO PRAY

Father, help me make the time in all the busyness of the next twenty-one days to set aside the never-ending distractions and give You the time and attention You rightly deserve. As I explore Colossians over the next few weeks, God, please give me a greater awe and love for You as I grow in my knowledge of who You are through Your Word. I pray that the Holy Spirit, who intercedes for me before You, Father, will help me understand Your Word more deeply, and ultimately, help me put Jesus first and at the center in my life. I ask that You guard me against making this devotional time just another thing to check off the list and accomplish but instead come to it daily so that I might meet with You and behold what YOU have accomplished already on my behalf through Christ. Reveal Yourself to me through Your Word, Lord, and let Your will be done in and through this devotional guide and in me as I journey through Colossians. Amen.

A BIRD'S-EYE VIEW

READ / *Colossians 1–4*

REFLECT / In all your excitement for a new adventure or social event, have you ever started on a journey somewhere without a clear, long look at the map first? I'm sure we've all done that at some point. Whether it's on a hike in the mountains or some leg of the journey in our personal lives, we've all made the mistake of taking steps before we know the lay of the land.

That can happen with the Bible sometimes, too. We can get so excited to dive into a specific passage, that we forget to see the larger picture it fits in. We forget it exists in a larger landscape—a context we'd be lost without. To help us avoid getting lost on our twenty-one-day journey through Colossians together, let's take today to consider the larger lay of the land before we walk through it. To get a bird's-eye view of Colossians (or any book of the Bible), here are some good questions we'll need to consider:

Who wrote it?

This question helps us identify the author, which for Colossians, is the apostle Paul. (More on him tomorrow!)

How was it written?

This question helps us identify the style of writing so that we might interpret it accordingly. Some books of the Bible were written as poetry or history or prophecy. The book of Colossians, though, is written as an "epistle," which just means it's a *letter*. Paul wrote several other letters found in the New Testament. Some of those include Romans, Galatians, Ephesians, 1 and 2 Corinthians, Philippians, and of course, one more of the thirteen letters Paul wrote, Colossians.

To whom was it written?

This question helps us identify the original audience of this letter and adds to our understanding of the writer's purpose. Having a better understanding of who this letter was originally written to helps us keep the letter within its proper context. This letter was written to the church in Colossae and addresses the current needs and issues happening within the church at the time. A unique aspect about this letter though is that Paul never visited this church. He received a report from a guy named Epaphras (Col. 1:7)—more on him later—who came to Rome to seek Paul's response on the false teaching that was starting to pop up in the church in Colossae. These false teachers were ultimately trying to diminish the sufficiency of Christ, meaning, they were teaching that other things were necessary for salvation *on top of* Christ's finished work on the cross. So, in this short letter written to the Colossians, Paul certainly and boldly responds to this issue. In every and any way, Paul declares that Jesus alone is sufficient and supreme over all things (*preeminent* is the big word he uses, as we'll see later).

When was it written?

This question helps us better understand the original audience's current experiences as Christians as they live during a certain time period. It's easy for us to picture the original audience as people who look and act just like you and me or live in a culture with the same norms as our culture. But asking the *when* question helps us pull them out of our moment in time, placing them back where they belong—within their own moment in history. For the book of Colossians, this was most likely around AD 62 while Paul was in prison in Rome.

Paul wrote this letter to the Colossians around the same time he penned his letter to Philemon and his letter to the Ephesians. Here are some other things happening during this time period that would be helpful to keep in mind as you study: this church, like many churches around this time period, was young (young is a loose word within this context, meaning they had only been around for five to ten—or maybe up to fifteen—years).

So, like many other churches that had been springing up, the Christians at the church in Colossae, are young. They are still immature, meaning they still have a lot of growing to do as believers. That's not a bad thing; it's just that they are still learning. When you're still learning something, you don't yet understand everything. You may make a mistake or get sidetracked. You may even be unable to tell the difference from what is correct and incorrect, true or false, because again, you're still learning about it. This was the case for the Colossians, which is part of the reason Paul is writing to them. He wants to help form them and grow them into Christlike maturity. This brings us to our last question to consider.

Why was it written?

This question helps us understand the situation that provoked the letter. As details in the letter reveal (and as many scholars help us see), Paul is writing to the church in Colossae because these young Christians need to be encouraged in the hope of the gospel, and they need to be reminded that the sufficiency of Christ always has been and always will be enough. Nothing could ever add to the completely finished work of Jesus to pay the price our sin required before a just and holy God. This young church needed to be reminded that nothing is greater in the life of the Christian than the surpassing worth of Christ. He is our highest joy. He is before all, above all, in all, and the Creator and Sustainer of all. He is the goal of creation. He is completely sufficient. He is first and best, greatest and highest. He is preeminent.

Jesus is the center of every single part of our lives, and who Jesus is has implications for every single part of our lives, too. Paul writes the words of this letter to the Colossians so they would not be led astray by the false teaching that has begun to take root in the church at this time and instead to hold fast to the hope they already have in Christ Jesus.

Man, isn't this exactly the reminder you and I need today? How easily we forget the sufficiency of Christ and instead of resting in His righteousness and the salvation we receive as a free gift through Him, we place our hope in lesser things or fall back into thinking that the only way to approach God is to follow a set of rules or do certain things in order to receive forgiveness from God. In a world full of distractions and desires that occupy our time and compete for our highest joy and centrality in our life, we need help to remember He is first and highest and central and worthy and ultimate and best. Thank You, Lord, for the book of Colossians that helps us remember the complete sufficiency and supremacy of Jesus! He is *enough*. And He is *higher* than all the other stuff that tries to distract us!

So there you have it. We've got our bird's-eye view—our bearings. We know the *who*, the *how*, the *when*, and the *why* surrounding this letter to the Colossians. We have a clearer picture of the terrain we're walking through together. Now that you have some background information, I'm going to ask you to do something you might call me crazy for—you ready?

Spend today (or various parts of today) reading this letter to the Colossians all the way through.

Nope, you didn't misread that. You read that right! Every day in this devotional, we will narrow in on one short passage, but *today's* task is to take the whole book into consideration. If that sounds intimidating to you, here are two pieces of great news. One, it's a super short book of the Bible. Only four quick chapters! You can do it. Whether you read it yourself or listen to it, or both, it won't take nearly as long as you think it will.

Two, reading the text will help us keep the big picture of the book within context. Think about it: if you or I were reading a letter we received from someone, they wouldn't want us to start randomly in the middle somewhere, right? They'd want us to read the whole letter, start to finish. In this way, it is helpful to read Colossians in the way it was intended to be read, which is all the way through.

If you start reading and don't understand something along the way, no worries. Just make a note of it and keep going. The goal is just to read it. In fact, I will encourage you a few more times throughout this journey to practice this technique called *repeated reading*. Think of this like moments in the journey where we stop, catch our breath, and look at the map again, reorienting ourselves to the big picture so that we can keep moving forward in confidence!

After you finish reading it once all the way through, give yourself a massive pat on the back and spend a short time in prayer, thanking God for His Word. Next, take some time to answer the reflection questions below to help you process what you've taken in. And then get ready—tomorrow we start breaking the big picture down, moving through our journey leg by leg.

RESPOND

1 / Have you ever gotten lost or felt disoriented in a new place where you didn't know the lay of the land? What was that like? How is this similar to reading Scripture without context?

2 / What fears do you have about reading large chunks of Scripture? What excites you about this?

3 / Now that you've read the book in its entirety, what are some themes or repeated ideas you noticed so far in the book of Colossians? What about God's character specifically stands out to you that you noticed after your first pass through the book of Colossians?

4 / What parts of your reading encouraged you? Challenged you?

5 / What places in your reading left you confused? Keep a list so that you can go back to your questions and answer them later, as you learn more.

Keep in Mind: There will be plenty of times in our Bible reading when we may not always get our questions answered right away. You may even have questions that do not get answered after you finish this devotional guide—that's okay! Reading the Bible over the long haul helps you here. You may read some other part of God's Word years from now that sheds light on some of the questions raised in this journey through Colossians. That's the beauty of the Bible—it is inexhaustible! As you read more of it over time, it offers greater clarity to the parts you were once foggy about. So don't be intimidated by questions—they are your friend, and you'll get answers to them as you grow over a lifetime. So ask the questions. Search the Scriptures for your answer where you can. Trust God and His character if your question goes unanswered for now, and trust Him to reveal that answer to you if that is His will and in His perfect timing. Then, keep going, sister.

PRAY

Heavenly Father, I thank You for your unchanging Word. I thank You for Your unchanging character. I thank You that through Christ I have been reconciled to You for all of eternity. I ask that as I continue forward in this journey through Colossians, You would give me eyes to clearly see Your character, the good news of the gospel, and the hope that Jesus offers. I pray that I would not just learn about You but grow to know You and love You more. In the name of Jesus, amen.

EXPLORE MORE

> *If you're up for it, or have extra time, consider these connections to shed some light on your reading:*

Read Psalm 98:3, and consider how it connects to what Colossians 1:5–6 says about the whole world.

Read Psalm 89:27 and Romans 8:29, and consider how these verses connect to Colossians 1:15.

Consider how John 1:1–3; John 8:58; Romans 11:36; and 1 Corinthians 8:6 relate to Colossians 1:16–17.

Consider how Genesis 3:15 and John 12:31 connect with Colossians 2:15.

Read Philippians 3:21 and 1 John 3:2, and consider how these passages help you better understand Colossians 3:4.

Consider how Exodus 30:35 sheds light on what "seasoned with salt" means in Colossians 4:6.

GOD CAN CHANGE ANYONE

READ / *Paul, an apostle of Christ Jesus by the will of God, and Timothy our brother, To the saints and faithful brothers in Christ at Colossae: Grace to you and peace from God our Father."*

—Colossians 1:1–2

REFLECT / I love Christmas. I love celebrating the birth of our Savior with my family—the Advent devotionals, the hymns and carols, the lights on the tree, the food, the wonder in my kids' eyes when baby Jesus is finally placed in our life-size wooden manger on Christmas morning where our nativity scene sits in our basement and we sing "Hark! The Herald Angels Sing" and other hymns gathered round on Christmas morning . . . and how could I forget the movies?

Speaking of movies, I'm sure you've seen *The Grinch*. When I was thinking about the life of Paul, oddly enough, that green guy from Whoville comes to mind. Stay with me here!

At the beginning of the story, the Grinch is a mean, grumpy, vile foe to the people of Whoville. He stands far above them on Mount Crumpit, judging them, seething against them, and seeking to destroy their dearly held tradition of Christmas—and really, the whole morale of the townspeople in general. He'd do anything and everything to thwart their plans to make Christmas happen.

But, as the story goes on, as the Grinch takes away everything he thinks the Whoville townspeople need in order to celebrate Christmas, he comes to a realization. Although he succeeded in agitating the people of Whoville and stealing all their Christmas *stuff*—the presents, the decorations, the food, the lights—he didn't steal Christmas itself. He couldn't stop it. Christmas came all the same. As he hears the joyful singing from the people in Whoville despite everything being taken away from them, he discovers that Christmas means much more than "stuff" to the people of Whoville. And by the end of the story, the Grinch's heart changed—it grew! He went from hating the Whoville townspeople and their Christmas holiday to loving them—even joining the townspeople in celebrating with them at their Christmas meal!

Do you remember who did the lion's share of changing the Grinch's mind along the way in his journey? A little girl named Cindy, who was willing to come close to him when no one else dared go near him. She snuck into his house and interrupted his life, challenging him to see things differently. She challenged him to come down from his high horse, get to know the people of Whoville, try out Christmas, and change. And it worked! In the ending scene of the movie, Cindy kisses the Grinch's cheek and notices a massive change: it's not cold and clammy anymore. It's warm. The cold Grinch changed to a warm member of the very group he once hated. He went from being Christmas's biggest threat to its greatest champion. All because of an unexpected visitor who interrupted his life up there on Mount Crumpit.

The book of Colossians is penned by a person with a (sort of) similar story. Still with me here? Paul (and his fellow worker in the gospel, Timothy) is writing to the Christians in Colossae. But who is Paul? What's his backstory? We tend to lift him up as a hero sometimes, given that he was appointed an apostle of Jesus, the author of thirteen of the twenty-seven New Testament books, and one of the most significant people in the history of the Christian faith. *But who was he before that?* Was he always one of the good guys?

No. He wasn't. Similar to the Grinch, Paul's heart was hardened and cold in many ways. He hated Christians and everything they stood for because their belief and faith in Jesus threatened everything he thought he knew about the Jewish Mosaic Law, which he was highly trained in. Before Jesus met Paul on the road to Damascus (Acts 9:1–9), and long before the letter to the Colossians was written, Paul was doing some pretty terrible things.

Paul was born in Tarsus with a Hebrew name—Saul. But because he had dual citizenship in Rome, he also went by a Roman name, Paul, after he was converted. Listen to how he describes who he used to be in Philippians 3: "Of the people of Israel, of the tribe of Benjamin, a Hebrew of Hebrews; as to the law, a Pharisee; as to zeal, a persecutor of the church; as to righteousness under the law, blameless" (vv. 5–6).

What's he saying? Paul says he used to be considered elite among the Pharisees (the religious top dogs of the Jews, highly trained as I mentioned a couple paragraphs above) and a persecutor and killer of Christians. Just a hair darker than the Grinch, but you see where I'm going with this, right? Like the Grinch, he stood far away from Christians, seething against them and judging them, getting them all wrong, and planning for the demise of their dearly held movement. He thought he was in the right to do this because he once believed he was blameless according to the Mosaic Law that the Pharisees clung to for peace with God. And he got Jesus all wrong. He thought Jesus wanted to dismiss the Law. Because Paul was spiritually dead, he was blinded from seeing and believing in the One who came not to abolish the Law but to fulfill it (Matt. 5:17; Rom. 5:1–11).

In Acts 9, there's somewhat of a showdown. While Paul is on his way to persecute Christians, the risen Christ, kind of like how Cindy shows up in *The Grinch*, graciously (but much more drastically!) interrupts Paul's plans for harm and converts him. A light from heaven shone all around Paul, causing him to fall to the ground. Jesus—who has died and is now resurrected—then begins speaking to Paul saying: "Saul, Saul, why are you persecuting me?" (v. 4). Saul responds, "Who are you, Lord?" and Jesus replies: "I am Jesus, whom you are persecuting" (v. 5). Saul wasn't just persecuting the *body* of Christ (the church); he was persecuting its *Head*—Jesus Himself! (Col. 1:18).

Jesus then tells Paul to rise, go to the city, and he will be told what to do next. Paul doesn't hesitate to listen to Jesus, but as he gets up, he cannot see anything. For three days he remained blind, but his sight eventually recovered. Can you imagine? Being on your way to *kill* Jesus's people, assuming their claims of His resurrection to be a lie, only to meet Jesus face-to-face with heaven's glory all around you, bringing you to your knees? Surely the Lord should have taken Paul out, right? But in His grace, He doesn't. Instead, He says this: "[Paul] is a chosen instrument of mine to carry my name before the Gentiles and kings and the children of Israel. For

I will show him how much he must suffer for the sake of my name" (Acts 9:15–16).

So, what do we learn from Paul's backstory? We learn that the chiefest of sinners can be converted into a chosen instrument of Jesus. Praise God! We learn that an agitator can be turned into an apostle. That a threat to the church can become its greatest champion. That a previous hater of the Gentiles and now current enemy of the Jews can be given authority to carry Jesus's name before both groups of people! That it really is possible to switch sides from darkness to light. *That God can change anyone.*

The Grinch had a life-altering heart transformation that completely changed his plans to destroy the Whoville townspeople and Christmas, all because a little girl dared to come close to him, interrupt him, and challenge him. In an infinitely greater way, Jesus came close to Paul when no one else would, interrupted his plans to snuff out Christians and the Great Commission (Matt. 28:16–20), and challenged him. Jesus doesn't just stop or challenge Paul's evil plans and mission; He immediately transforms Paul's heart. Instead of seeking to follow his own way, Paul follows Jesus and trusts Him completely. Blinded and humbled, Paul is made low and rightly sees Jesus where He's already seated at the right hand of the Father: the goal of creation, sufficient and supreme above everything else, the eternal King and Savior of the world, preeminent. There's that big word again! And just like that, the cold, seething Pharisee becomes the warmest member of a group he once hated.

When we look at Paul's story, it becomes clear: only God can do that. Only by the power of the Holy Spirit can a spiritually dead person who is blinded by sin be made alive together with Christ

(Col. 1:21–22), scales removed from their eyes, entering from the domain of darkness into His marvelous light. Only God can save a sinner like Paul; . . . only God can save a sinner like you and me. If God can save a man like Saul, He can save anyone. If God can save a woman like me, He can save anyone. That's encouraging!

And you know what? God doesn't just stop there by saving Paul. He uses Paul to do amazing things. For starters, immediately after his conversion, Paul begins proclaiming Jesus in the very city he had originally intended to persecute Christians! Paul's highest joy has dramatically shifted away from his own self-righteousness to the righteousness of Christ alone, and that changed everything. Paul realized that Jesus alone is worthy of all of his worship. Paul not only receives Christ; he begins walking in Him immediately by proclaiming Christ publicly and writing about Christ in his letters to churches—one of which is Colossians. What does this mean for our twenty-one-day journey through Colossians? It means that as we read every word, we should keep in mind the backstory of the man who is writing it. We should remember that the words of this letter aren't written by some perfect person who always got everything right and expects you to get things right in your own strength. No—quite the opposite, actually—it's written by someone who knows what it's like to get it wrong, to experience lavish grace, and to walk in the grace of new life given through Christ. It's written by someone who wants to point you to the only One who had power to change and save him—to the only One who holds the power to save and change you and me by His justifying work on the cross and by His resurrection. To the only One who continues to change us more and more to the likeness of Himself for the rest of our lives (Phil. 1:6). That only One, Jesus Christ the righteous. So, when you are challenged or interrupted by something you read, or if you feel deeply convicted by something you come across, remember Paul's story and believe that God can change anyone, *including you. (And including that person you ache for to turn from their sin and turn to and trust in Jesus!)* Jesus changed the writer of Colossians, and He can change you, the reader. He can move you from cold to warm!

Step-by-step in our journey through this letter, we will see this changed Paul echoing the themes of his conversion, the ones that left a mark on him forever: Jesus is the highest and best. The alpha and the omega, the first and the last, the beginning and the end (Rev. 21:6; 22:13). Jesus is the center and focal point of everything in all of creation now. And He's not these things just for today—He is and will be these things forever. All of history is moving toward the day when, in the end the entire created universe will bring glory to Him and dwell with God forever (Rev. 21:1–7). Given all this, it's clear: Jesus alone is worthy of all of our worship, sister, and receiving Jesus always results in a life that walks in Him afterward.

Meet me here tomorrow, and we'll look closer at how Paul's first words in this letter reveal something we should all be marked by as Christians—gratitude. See you then, friend!

RESPOND

1 / Knowing the context now of who Paul was before he was converted, what does that teach you about God's ability to save a person? What does this show you about His attributes (what He is like)? Reference the attributes of God listed in the back of this book to help you answer these questions.

2 / Although the formal office of apostle is no longer needed, have you ever considered yourself someone God is "sending" to others? Or perhaps as an "instrument" of God's work in the world? Why or why not? How might seeing yourself this way change how you view your purpose in your home, workplace, and wider relationships?

3 / Is there anyone on your heart right now whom you love who has not trusted in Jesus—who seems too "bad" or coldhearted or far off for God to save? How does the life of Paul encourage you and change the way you view God's ability to save that person?

PRAY

Thank You, God, for Your powerful ability to save Your people. Thank You, God, for interrupting my life and saving me! I was once just as blind as Paul, but You opened my eyes, and now I can see. I praise You right now for taking me from being separated from Your people to being brought in, a member of Your family and the community of the church. And if You can do that for me, You can do it for anyone! I pray for the people on my heart today who don't know Jesus as Lord—help me believe You love them even more than I do and that You are able to save them. I surrender their story to You, the only One who can change their cold hearts and turn them warm for You. I pray this over my children, family, neighbors, friends, and coworkers, Lord. Help me live as one who is sent out into the world by You, an instrument of Your hands, bearing the name of Christ and helping others come to know You. I pray for grace and peace within my heart, my home, my church, my marriage, my workplace, my children, my extended family, my community, my state, and my country. In the name of Jesus, amen.

Consider the full account of Saul and his conversion in Acts 6–9. What stands out most to you?

Read Romans 4:13–25. What do you learn about the faith of Abraham in these verses? What do you learn about the faithfulness of God to Abraham? Why was Abraham's faith counted to him as righteousness? Why is our faith counted to us as righteousness now?

Read Romans 5:1–11. Define justified. *What does it mean to be justified by faith? How do we have peace with God?*

GOSPEL GRATITUDE

READ / *We always thank God, the Father of our Lord Jesus Christ, when we pray for you, for we have heard of your faith in Christ Jesus and of the love you have for all the saints because of the hope reserved for you in heaven. You have already heard about this hope in the word of truth, the gospel that has come to you. It is bearing fruit and growing all over the world, just as it has among you since the day you heard it and came to truly appreciate God's grace. You learned this from Epaphras, our dearly loved fellow servant. He is a faithful minister of Christ on your behalf, and he has told us about your love in the Spirit.*

—Colossians 1:3–8 CSB

REFLECT / Fear, cynicism, misinformation. Is it just me, or do you see these things everywhere you cast your eyes these days? It doesn't take long to look around and realize that we live in a broken world. A world that since the fall (Gen. 3) has been cursed by the entrance of sin. When we look around at our culture and even in our own hearts, we see a failure to love one another as we should, to obey God's Word, and to reject the idols of this world that entice us and distract us from worshipping the one, true God. We see lies instead of truth. We see pain from hurtful words and actions. We see pride and jealousy and division.

Maybe it's because I'm a mom of littles, but it all reminds me of that Disney movie kids everywhere have been raving about since the day it came out: *Frozen*. If you've seen this movie, you know how bleak the situation was. On the inside of the castle walls, the two main characters—sisters Elsa and Anna—had all sorts of built-up angst between the two of them. They needed a heart change. And on the outside, their kingdom was just as messed up. They faced a lying prince trying to steal the seat of power and a greedy trading community that wanted to underhandedly take all the goods of their kingdom. Coldness was the norm everywhere they looked.

And then, in bebops a warmhearted creature full of otherworldly thankfulness: Olaf the snowman. In even the darkest scenes, Olaf is there in stark contrast to everyone else, radiating gratitude for some small, seemingly insignificant, thing. When push comes to shove, that peculiar little snowman always seems to be marked by gratitude, and his thankfulness is contagious, changing the outlook of the people around him.

For the Christian, there is a greater hope for both our broken hearts and the broken world we live in. In the incredibly difficult and dark circumstances we face in this world, Christians have a unique opportunity to be the Olafs of the world—better yet, to be the Christlike people in this world—who are marked by a gratitude that radiates outward everywhere we go. And I don't mean just any sort of gratitude but one that is rooted in the gospel. A gospel that transforms hearts, a gospel that is true, and a gospel that is contagious, multiplying out to the end of the earth—just as Jesus commanded His disciples to do in the Great Commission (Matt. 28:16–20).

That's what we see happening in these opening words of Paul's letter to the Colossians. We see him practicing what it means to be marked by gratitude, despite the persecution and imprisonment he and those he is writing to are currently facing. He could have been fearful or cynical, given the situation he was in. Yet here is an unexpected, bright ray of gospel gratitude that shines into the difficulty and the darkness: "We always thank God . . ."

But for what, exactly? What is Paul thankful for? For the gospel that has transformed the hearts and lives of the Colossians, for their faith in Christ, for the love they show for other believers (despite their differences and despite the fact that the world tells them they shouldn't!), for the hope that is laid up in heaven for them, and for the fact that the gospel is bearing fruit not only in their community but all over the world (1:3–6).

If Paul is *this* enthusiastic and expectant about the gospel being received, we should pause and double-check something—what *is* the gospel exactly? What is this message he's so eager for people to receive? It's the message about Jesus's life, death on the cross for all sin, and resurrection. See, to be accepted before God, we must live a perfect, sinless, life. But we can't. Not one of us is perfect, not a single one (Rom. 3:23)! But Jesus was perfect and completely sinless; therefore, He lived a perfect life on our behalf so that we might have something to stand on before God—a perfect record. And in His death, He paid the penalty for all the ways we've failed to live up to perfection. He lived perfectly in our place, *and* He died perfectly in our place so that we might be accepted before God. And what's more—Jesus didn't just die; He resurrected, taking on our greatest enemy (death) and winning! Because Christ defeated sin and death victoriously, those who have trusted in Christ will be raised to life with Him, too (2 Tim. 2:11; Rom. 6:8). Meaning, one day we'll resurrect from the grave just as He did and live forever with Him. We will have ultimate victory over our sin and over death, not by anything we do to try to earn it, but only because of what Christ has already accomplished for us, and that is good news for you and me!

Paul is so eager he radiates gratitude because these Colossians not only say they *believe* this gospel message; they are *acting like it* in the way they love one another! And more, they have an eternal hope for their future.

What gets you eager about sharing something or doing something? In your most grateful moment, what floods you with thankfulness and excitement? While many things can produce gratitude in us, Paul's words here in Colossians challenge us. He shows us what we should be *most* thankful about, and it's not the things *we* receive, but instead it's about *others* receiving and living out the gospel.

When you think of what you're most thankful for today, who are the "Colossians" for you? Which people do you point at and say, "I'm thankful for a lot of things, but I'm most thankful that you know the gospel and you're living it out in the way you love others. I'm *most* thankful that because of His grace, you'll experience resurrection life with Jesus! And I'm even more thankful that the message you believe is being circulated around the globe right now!" I need to hear this challenge from Paul. You, too?

As we walk through trials, disappointments, confusion, misinformation, and suffering of various kinds in this world that can cause us to lose sight of what we are to be most thankful for, let us be that peculiar, otherworldly person who is marked by the gratitude Paul exemplifies in this passage for us. Let us, as Paul will go on to say later in this letter, put on the new self as those who are now a new creation in Christ, "as God's chosen ones, holy and beloved" (Col. 3:12–17).

Friend, let us hold fast to the good news of the gospel, for it will anchor us as we navigate living in a broken world. And friend, let us look up, look around, and see all that God is accomplishing as He advances the gospel in our own lives and in the lives of those around us. When the world rolls in with its typical cynicism and fear, let's be warm and radiant in a refreshing posture of thanks, and when we're asked why, let's make clear that we're most thankful for the fact that the glorious gospel of Jesus is doing its work, saving souls and bearing fruit in the lives of those we love and all around the world. Jesus came to save sinners! This, friend, is the good news worthy of all of our praise, worship, and gratitude to God, for all of our days. Let us be marked by this beautiful good news. Amen?

RESPOND

1 / What's the difference between *general* gratitude and *gospel* gratitude? Do you beam with the kind of gospel gratitude Paul radiates in this passage? Why or why not?

2 / What does today's passage teach you about God's character? How can you live in response to this part of His character today? Because God is _____, I will _____.

3 / How would you put the message of the gospel in your own words?

4 / What example does Paul give us in how we ought to pray for one another?

5 / In what specific ways can you be marked by gospel gratitude this week? (Idea: As you think about your relationships, in whose life is the gospel doing great work right now, and how might you express thanks or encouragement to that person this week?)

PRAY

Thank You, Jesus my Savior, for the gospel—the message of hope that is spreading across the whole world! Thank You, Jesus, for this good news to sinners like me. Thank You for living a sinless life in my place and also dying on the cross in my place, too, for sin you never committed. And thank You for the resurrection—that You didn't stay dead but rose victoriously three days later over sin and death. Thank You for the promise that means for me and all those who trust in You that we will one day be raised to life with You! I pray You'll instill in me the kind of gratitude that radiates outward, shining light into a confused and chaotic world, and I pray that You'll make me most thankful for the gospel's power in the lives of others and in my own life, too. In Your name, amen.

As we've seen, Paul opens his letter with thankfulness to God and this gospel gratitude, but this will not be the last time these things are mentioned. Read Colossians 3:15–16. What are the Colossians to be thankful for? For what reason should their hearts be full of gratitude?

In both the Old and New Testament, showing thankfulness to God is mentioned over and over again (for example, Psalms 100; 107; 145; 150:6; Isaiah 12:4; Ephesians 5:18–20; Hebrews 13:15–16; and Revelation 11:16–17). When we read the Bible and see repetition of an idea, a theme, or a phrase (in our case, thankfulness), what do you think is God's point or purpose for doing so? (Hint: think about it from a mother's perspective. Why would you repeat something over and over again to your child? What point or for what purpose are you trying to make to them through that repetition?)

FILLED WITH EVEN
MORE FRUIT

READ / *And so, from the day we heard, we have not ceased to pray for you, asking that you may be filled with the knowledge of his will in all spiritual wisdom and understanding, so as to walk in a manner worthy of the Lord, fully pleasing to him: bearing fruit in every good work and increasing in the knowledge of God; being strengthened with all power, according to his glorious might, for all endurance and patience with joy; giving thanks to the Father, who has qualified you to share in the inheritance of the saints in light.*

—*Colossians 1:9–12*

REFLECT / As a mom of young children, I enjoy spending time with my kids outside for some fresh air and to take in God's creation during our stroller walks. We live in Minnesota, where the weather can get cold many months of the year, so our warm spring and summer days are a treasure. I strap the kids in and we walk.

There is something about the sustained forward progress, the fresh air, and the gentle movement in the stroller that is the perfect combination for my little ones (and their mama) to squeeze in a little mental break during our day, and it really resets all of us.

If you were to define the word *walk*, I bet you'd think of things like this: to move, to go, to advance, to trudge, to stride. And you'd be right. These definitions are in many dictionaries. And I love how descriptive those last two definitions are, don't you? They offer such a range of what walking can feel like. Some days walking feels like taking big, easy strides. Other days it feels like a trudge. Maybe you can relate.

As we saw yesterday, Paul has just thanked God for the ways the gospel is bearing fruit in the lives of these Colossian believers (and the way the gospel message is spreading all over the world). In this next leg of our journey through Colossians, Paul moves on to pray for the spiritual growth of these believers.

It's as if he's saying this: *I heard about all the fruit the gospel is bearing in your life. I'm so thankful for it, and now I pray for it to bear even more fruit. I know you're healthy, but I pray that you won't stop there. I pray you won't stop growing. I pray the good work God is doing in your midst increases even more.*

Paul can't hold his desire back for these Colossian believers that Paul hasn't even met in-person before! But he's heard about them and the good work God is doing in them. He deeply longs for their forward progress in the gospel. So, he begs God to continue His ongoing work in their hearts to make them more like Jesus—a process called *sanctification*. Paul sees the fruit, and he's grateful, but he also wants this fruit to mature over time.

So, what are the markers of this growth? What are the specific areas where Paul wants them—and us—to grow as we mature in our faith?

First, he wants them to know that they can't fill themselves with good spiritual fruit. No, they have to "*be* filled." That means God is the One who does the filling! Isn't that a relief? We certainly have to cooperate with God as He matures us, but ultimately, He's the one who fills us with more and more fruit. *He's* the one who takes what is there and grows it into more.

But grows us in *what*, exactly? What will God fill us with? What are the ways we should be growing? Paul tells us: knowledge, wisdom, good works, strength, patience, endurance, and joy—to name a few!

Wonderful. But why did the Colossians—and why do we—need to be filled with these things? What's the point? Paul tells us: so that we can continue "to walk in a manner worthy of the Lord, fully pleasing to him" (Col. 1:10). God is pleased when we are abounding in good fruit—when we are spiritually growing—and so God does the work to grow us and to please Himself. Isn't that great news? God is pleased with fruitfulness in His creatures. And so, to satisfy Himself, He will make us fruitful. *He* will fill us. All we have to do, like Paul, is ask.

The Christian life is a call to walk obediently with Christ and increasingly bear good fruit from the inside out. And if you're wondering what good fruit looks like, in another letter to a different church, Paul describes it as "love, joy, peace, patience, kindness, goodness, faithfulness, gentleness, and self-control" (Gal. 5:22–23). Bearing fruit is Paul's call to the Colossians as they face persecution of various kinds and false teaching. This is also the call for you and me as followers of Jesus.

As we walk forward, some days this sanctification process of growth may feel like a stride. Some days it may feel like a trudge, and that's okay too. The work of growing doesn't always feel good (like gardening, fruitfulness requires clipping and pruning and hot rays of sun), but it is always for our good that God continues to work in us, continues to show us our sin, continues to convict our hearts, and continues to change our sinful desires to fruitful desires that please and glorify God. Even on the days that feel more like a trudge, may we remember who is at work in us even through our growing pains in our faith and that, in Christ, *God* is the one who fills us with good fruit and gives us the power to joyfully walk in obedience with Him, even when sanctification feels hard or slow. God calls us all to maturity in Christ, even when it's hard or slow, and by His grace, we *can*, we *do*, and we *will* grow in spiritual maturity as believers. As Paul reminds us in another one of his letters: "He who began a good work in you *will* bring it to completion" (Phil. 1:6, emphasis mine). Praise God!

And friend, don't miss how this section of Colossians closes: The Father Himself has *qualified* you to participate in all of this growth through His Son's work. You didn't qualify yourself to come into the blessings of God's family, where He helps His children grow in obedience and fruitfulness. Jesus's work brought you in. You're qualified because of *Him*, and you'll grow because of Him. What good news! This is just another beautiful truth that proves Jesus really is highest and best—something Paul refers to as Jesus's "preeminence," as we'll see in just a few short verses from now. You're qualified through Christ, and He's made it possible for you to grow by the power of His Spirit, the Holy Spirit! What a strong and beautiful reason to put Him first in our lives, friend.

If you are bearing fruit today in Christ, if you're walking forward, uphill or down, celebrate this! And then, like Paul, ask God to fill you with even more fruit and all the obedience you need to take another step!

RESPOND

1 / Paul is already pleased and thankful for the obvious spiritual fruit in the lives of the Colossians, and yet he prays for more. If he were to evaluate your spiritual fruit (or your forward progress in obedience to God), what would his findings be? Why?

2 / How can we, like Paul says, increase in our knowledge of God?

3 / Is there anyone in your life whose spiritual growth you forget to pray for simply because they are already bearing good fruit in the Lord? How does today's passage challenge this?

4 / In what specific ways can you walk in a manner worthy of the Lord, fully pleasing to Him this week? Asked another way, is there anything you need to keep doing that is clearly *helping* you bear fruit? Is there anything you need to stop doing because it is clearly *hindering* your growth toward Christian maturity and obedience to God? How will you take steps toward this?

5 / What does today's passage teach you about God's character? How can you live in response to this part of His character today? Because God is _____, I will _____.

PRAY

Lord, I thank You for who You are. You are the One who fills me—who makes me fruitful! I thank You for the work You've already done in my life, and I pray along with Paul that You would fill me even more—with knowledge, wisdom, understanding, endurance, patience, and strength. Help me keep growing in the Spirit's fruit of love, joy, peace, patience, kindness, goodness, faithfulness, gentleness, and self-control, both internally and externally. Take what You've already done in me, and grow it into more! Help me be obedient and walk each day in a manner worthy of You, Lord, so that I might bear fruit in every good work. And give me eyes to see those around me whom You want me to keep praying for, even if they are already fruitful to some measure. I know You are cultivating the faith of the people coming to my mind right now—help me remember to pray for them more often as they grow. Amen.

One of the themes woven throughout the book of James is spiritual maturity ("spiritual maturity" is just another way of saying fruitfulness in the life of a Christian). As James writes this short letter, we see him lay out portraits of what Christian maturity looks like. Read through the entire letter (just five short chapters!) and make note of the different ways James calls the Christian to maturity.

Read 1 John 5:1–5. Why is the call to obey God's commandments not a burden to the Christian? Should our obedience to God be out of duty or out of love for God, or both?

Look up the following examples in Scripture of God calling His people to walk in obedience with Him (which leads to a life of fruitfulness). Make note of whom God calls, what He calls them to do, and what cost or price was necessary in order to obey God's commands. You may not be able to get to all of these today, but if you're able, trust me: seeing the faithfulness of God to His people from Genesis to Revelation will encourage your heart as you see how God's faithfulness to call us and grow us into obedient followers has nothing to do with us and everything to do with Him.

Genesis 3:1–12   *Genesis 6:11–22*
Genesis 12:1–9   *Exodus 3*
Isaiah 43:1–7   *Jeremiah 1:4–9*
Matthew 10:1–4   *2 Timothy 1:1–14*
1 Peter 2:9   *Hebrews 1:1–4*
Revelation 21:1–5

WHY JESUS DESERVES
TO BE FIRST

READ / *He has delivered us from the domain of darkness and transferred us to the kingdom of his beloved Son, in whom we have redemption, the forgiveness of sins.*

He is the image of the invisible God, the firstborn of all creation. For by him all things were created, in heaven and on earth, visible and invisible, whether thrones or dominions or rulers or authorities—all things were created through him and for him. And he is before all things, and in him all things hold together. And he is the head of the body, the church. He is the beginning, the firstborn from the dead, that in everything he might be preeminent. For in him all the fullness of God was pleased to dwell, and through him to reconcile to himself all things, whether on earth or in heaven, making peace by the blood of his cross.

—Colossians 1:13–20

REFLECT / I have always loved a good competition. I grew up loving to play sports (namely, soccer), and I have always loved watching sports of all kinds. Prior to becoming a Christian, as someone who grew up most of her childhood and college years identifying as an "athlete," I grew to love that title. When being introduced to another person (or any time I had the chance, really), I would find a way to slide in my elevated title as a top athlete in my high school, or if the conversation centered around college memories, I'd always make sure to include some kind of evidence that I had extended my soccer career past high school, mentioning my more formal title as "student athlete." I loved that title. And if someone didn't know about it already, I loved making sure they were made aware by the end of our conversation. Deep down, I loved the praise of others. I loved my identity as being an athlete more than just about anything else.

But my love for these things ultimately would lead to my loss.

Sports, competing, roles and titles God's given us to live out for His glory—these things are not bad in and of themselves. But for me they had become a major problem in my life because athleticism wasn't just a hobby to me. It was everything. It was my identity. Soccer clearly had moved past being one of many things in my life I loved to being *ultimate*. It no longer held a proper place in my heart because it was elevated above my love for Jesus. And as you probably know, when this happens, it leads to even greater issues like pridefulness, idolatry, and false security. But in reality, that sin and other issues noted above were already there, soccer just brought those things out of me.

For the Colossians reading Paul's letter, and for you and me today, our relationship with Jesus can take a similar turn. We can easily forget who Jesus is and where His rightful place should be in our hearts and in our lives. This forgetfulness leads to us allowing other things to creep in and take up first place in our hearts and lives.

See, some of the Colossians have taken on a spirituality that has started to allow other things (even good things!) to creep in and compete with their love for Jesus. Paul's greatest concern isn't that they would completely abandon Christ, but that they would forget all that He is for them and grow apathetic toward Him over time. Think of it like this: "I love _____. Oh, and I love Jesus, too."

Some of these Colossians would have filled that blank with a few things they considered highest and best. For some this was the idolatry of knowledge, which makes us think that Christianity is merely competency in the right things. But when accumulation of knowledge becomes the end goal instead of knowledge being a means by which our lives are transformed by the gospel, we get it wrong. For others, it looked like the idolatry of self—the idea that we are self-sufficient and that everyone else exists to give us what we think we deserve. In today's world that message comes across as "I'm enough." For others, it looked like following the right Jewish rules—the idea that if we just obey enough of the Law, we'll be accepted before God. And for still others, it looked like making the Jesus of the Bible into a Jesus we like better—Jesus we prefer, one we're comfortable with, one we can manipulate. A Jesus who exists to make us happy as we define happiness.

Except, the more and more we elevate these things in our hearts as highest, looking to ourselves or other things to fulfill us, the emptier we become. We're losing, badly. The only one who can truly satisfy our weary and searching souls is Jesus. The only one who can transform us is Jesus. We, like the Colossians, can be so quick to forget this. It reminds me a lot of the forgetfulness of the Israelites after God freed them from their bondage of slavery in Egypt and led them in the wilderness for forty years to the Promised Land. Over and over, the Israelites forgot their God and looked back at their "comforts" they had in Egypt . . . as slaves! How twisted our view of things becomes when we forget God.

Paul wants them to keep Jesus as first and highest in their hearts and lives because of how easy it is to elevate other things to His level. Paul is concerned they will allow something else to fill in the blank before Christ, and that just can't be so for the Christian! It can't be so for you and me, friend. We will only feel empty if we do that. We must always put Jesus first above everything else.

Here's the good news for us. Paul doesn't just say, "Put Jesus first already!" without further explanation. He doesn't just tell them what to do and then walk away. Instead, he helps them put Jesus first by telling them *why*. He lays out a clear and right view of who Jesus is and who He should be in the lives of the Colossian believers and in our own lives too. He reminds them that Jesus must be the most central part of our lives as Christians *because of all that He is for us*. He must be our greatest joy. He must be better than anything and everything else in our life—yes, even the best things (including people!) you can think of—because of *who He is* compared to all those things. When we look at who Jesus really is and what He has done for us, we will keep Him first and best in our lives, and in turn, that will orient everything and everyone else rightly. It is for our good and God's glory that we keep Him first and highest. Praise God!

So, who is Jesus? And how should we relate to Him? What reasons does Paul give for us to keep Him first and best next to all the other options out there?

First, *Christ is King* (1:13). Did you notice that Paul says we've been transferred not just into a state of freedom but into Jesus's *kingdom*? *Jesus* is the King of the kingdom we weren't naturally citizens of but had to be delivered into. We were once in the kingdom of darkness, but now we're in God's kingdom, all thanks to the work of Christ alone. We are now citizens of *heaven* (Phil. 3:20). And now that we're there, we should treat Jesus as King! Jesus deserves first place in your life because His work made it possible for you to be delivered from darkness to light and become a citizen of the kingdom that belongs to *Him*.

Second, *Christ is your Redeemer* (1:14). Notice how Paul says we don't just have redemption in general; we have redemption *in Him*. What does this mean? To redeem means to buy back. You were redeemed, bought back, with a price. And that price is Jesus's own body and blood, which paid for your sins. Your redemption was something not just given but *purchased* by Jesus so that your sins would be paid for and forgiven, which is another reason He deserves to be highest and best in your life!

Third, *Jesus is the "image of the invisible God"* (1:15). In other words, the visible man named Jesus is the exact imprint of our invisible God, the fullness of God's deity dwelling in Him (Heb. 1:3; Col. 1:19; 2:9). We are all looking for images of what God is like, aren't we? Scripture tells us what God is like in two ways: through His written Word (the Bible) and through the living Word (Jesus Christ). If you're thinking, *I wonder what God would be like if He were a person walking around on earth*, Jesus Christ is the answer! He is the exact imprint of God (Heb. 1:3). He is the second Person of the Trinity who exists as Father, Son, and Holy Spirit. Friend, Jesus deserves to be first in your life because Jesus is God.

Fourth, *Jesus is the "firstborn of all creation"* (1:15). In the culture at the time, monarchs gave all their inheritance, rights, and privileges to their firstborn son. So, what is Paul is saying? That our heavenly Father has handed His Son, Jesus Christ, total dominion over the earth. The Father has handed the reins of everything and everyone in this world—including you and me!—over to His one and only Son. In other words, Jesus inherits all creation, because He is preeminent over all of creation. He is first and best over all of creation—which includes you and me!

Fifth, *Christ is Creator and Sustainer of the universe* (1:16–17). Doesn't this blow your mind? Christ wasn't just given dominion over the universe by happenstance; He *deserves* rulership over the universe because He's the One who created it and sustains it. In the Bible, one of the first things we learn about God is that He is the Creator of all things (Gen. 1), and that the way He created all things is through His Word. The Gospel of John tells us exactly who this "Word" is—Jesus (John 1:1–14). So when we read the story of creation, we should read it with eyes that see that the Word of God—Christ—is the One who built the world and formed man out of dust (Gen. 2:7). As we keep reading in the Gospels, we see that Jesus proves He is, indeed, the Creator who reigns supreme over His creation, as we watch Him calm a storm (Luke 8:22–25), heal the man with the demon (Mark 5:1–20), and heal Jairus's daughter (Mark 5:35–43)—all with just a word. Here we see so clearly that He upholds the universe by the *word* of His power (Heb. 1:3). Whether it is the realm of the seen or unseen, animate humans or inanimate elements of nature, Jesus is Lord over it. So, friend, Jesus deserves to be highest and best in your life because

He made you and He holds your very being together by His power, too.
Which is to say, sister, there is nothing going on in your life that
Jesus isn't absolutely in control of. There's nothing Jesus isn't big-
ger, greater, or stronger than. There's no realm His power does not
extend to. That's good news!

Sixth, *Jesus is the head of the church* (1:18). Jesus isn't just the Ruler
of a place (the world); He's the Ruler of a people (the church). If
you're a Christian, you are part of His people, and He loves to lead,
direct, guide, and nourish you as you walk in Him. He deserves to
be highest and best to you, because He's the head of the body you
are a member of.

Seventh, *Jesus is the guarantee of your future resurrection* (1:18).
Paul calls Jesus the "firstborn from the dead," meaning that He was
the first and only person to rise from the realm of the dead in His
own power, and once He defeated death in His own grave, He took
away death's power to keep *you* in the grave, too. Because Jesus rose
first, His resurrection guarantees the future resurrections of His
brothers and sisters that will follow. Jesus resurrected not merely
to defeat death for Himself but also to defeat it for you! He proved
Himself not just Lord of the earth but Lord of life and death itself!
It's no surprise, then, that Paul calls him "preeminent" because in
the resurrection on the other side of glory, He will be highest and
supreme, ruling over all, including all those who are resurrected in
His name (Rev. 19:6–10).

Eighth, *Jesus is a reconciler* (1:20). Though we were once at odds
with Him and the Father, He made peace through the blood of
His cross. He has reconciled us to the Father, and He will one
day reconcile the whole world to Himself! He deserves to be

most important to you because, although He could have come to *condemn* you before the Father, He came to *reconcile* you to the Father instead! Where He could've made war, He made peace. What good news!

If you, like me, are tempted to make Jesus everything you'd *prefer* Him to be while forgetting who He *actually* is—or if you're tempted to put something else as highest and best in your life, remember this loud and clear: Christ is the divine Creator of all things, Sustainer of all things, Inheritor of all things, and He alone holds the power to not only reconcile all things to Himself but *raise the dead* to live with Him in resurrection life forever. He's King.

Just think of the list of your "lesser loves" that might creep in to compete with Him—can you say any of these things about that lesser love? Of course not! Which tells you what? That Jesus is above them. Jesus is stronger than them. Jesus offers more joy than them. Jesus alone is worthy of all of our worship. He alone is our only hope in life and in death. He is first. He is highest. He is best. Allowing anything to take His place is exactly what Paul warns us against as we read the words he wrote to the Colossians. Apathy and forgetfulness are just as much a threat to us as they were to them. So, friend, when (not if) that threat comes creeping into your life, return to this list in Colossians and *remember who Jesus truly is*.

I need this reminder just as much as anyone else. My hope is that today our love for Jesus might increase as we grow to know Him through God's Word. I pray we will lay down the things in our life that are competing with our love for Jesus and make Him the center, highest, and best once again. I pray God will continue to make us look more like His Son as we consistently practice putting Him first in our lives. Because He deserves it! There's no one like Jesus!

RESPOND

1 / Of the ways Jesus is described in this passage, which is new to you? Most encouraging to you? Most challenging? Why?

2 / Describe in your own words what it means when the passage says that "in everything he might be preeminent?"

3 / What in your life right now (maybe even good things) is competing for first place in your life? What specific things do you sometimes love more than Jesus? Write them down here; then confess this list to God in prayer. Ask God to help you lay those things down and put Jesus above them all in your heart and in your life.

4 / In Jesus, "all the fullness of God was pleased to dwell, and through him to reconcile to himself all things, making peace by the blood of His cross" (v. 19). Why is this good news for you?

5 / What does today's passage teach you about God's character? How can you live in response to this part of God's character today? Because God is _____, I will _____.

PRAY

Jesus, I stand amazed at all You are for me and for the world. I praise You for being the Creator of all things, including me. I thank You for holding all things together in Your great power as King. I thank You for Your redeeming blood shed on the cross, for it has reconciled me to You and the Father, and one day, it will reconcile all things to You! I thank You for defeating death so that one day I will resurrect into new life with You. I repent of the things I have allowed to creep into my heart and compete with my love for You. None of them compare to you! Continue to reveal those things to me, as they can quickly make me forget You. I pray that You'll help me make You my highest joy and the center of my life. Help me remember who You truly are, today and every day. In your name, amen.

Look closer at Mark 4:35–41. How does Jesus show us who God is in this passage when Jesus calms the storm? What does this passage tell us about the nature and characteristics of who Jesus (God!) is?

Our God is a God who speaks. He spoke creation into being, He spoke to Abraham, Isaac, Jacob, Noah, Moses, and prophets like Daniel and Jeremiah. But the greatest revelation (which is just a fancy way of saying how God has spoken or revealed something to us), is through His Son, Jesus (Heb. 1:1–3). Jesus is the greatest revelation to us that shows us what God is like. Think back to today's passage. In it we read that Jesus is the exact image of God (Col. 1:15). Now read Hebrews 1:3. Jesus is exactly like God. We don't have to wonder what God is like because He has already told us what He is like through His Word and His Son. Knowing this, if someone (maybe a friend or your child) were to ask you what God is like, how would you explain to them how you can, in fact, know God?

REMEMBER THE HOPE
OF THE GOSPEL

READ / *And you, who once were alienated and hostile in mind, doing evil deeds, he has now reconciled in his body of flesh by his death, in order to present you holy and blameless and above reproach before him, if indeed you continue in the faith, stable and steadfast, not shifting from the hope of the gospel that you heard, which has been proclaimed in all creation under heaven, and of which I, Paul, became a minister.*

—Colossians 1:21–23

REFLECT / Have you read through the The Chronicles of Narnia book series? One character's story has always stood out to me—Edmund's. His story has a theme of reconciliation. And as we look at Paul finishing his opening prayer for spiritual growth among these young Christians at the church in Colossae, we see a similar theme at play.

If we recall Edmund's story, we remember that it seemed like—outside looking in—that he was "part of the family." But the truth was, he was alienated from it. He may have had proximity to his family and traveled along with them, but in the world of his own mind, he was hostile toward his brothers and sisters (and even Aslan), and he did evil deeds because of his hard heart. But Aslan, by payment of his own body on the stone table, ended up reconciling Edmund to himself and to his family. He was once alienated and hostile, but now he's brought near and he's kinder. There's a scene where he goes into the tent with Aslan, they have a conversation, and when they emerge, Edmund is released from his debt. Though he once carried all the blame, he is now cleared and presented to the White Witch as blameless. All because of Aslan's plan to physically sacrifice himself on Edmund's behalf and bear Edmund's blame.

Surely Edmund can't forget what has happened to him, right? Going forward, the test for Edmund will be if he can remember the truth—that Aslan gave up his own body so that he might be free and reconciled and no longer hostile. He must hold on to the good news of what Aslan did and walk in light of it.

Paul wraps up his prayer by reminding the Colossians, and us, of similar themes we see in Edmund's experience. He reminds us who we once were apart from Christ and who we are now. As former unbelievers, those not in Christ, we were once alienated, like Edmund was—at odds with God and our spiritual family. Like Edmund, we were hostile in our ways and in our minds. Such was true of us before we trusted in Christ. As Romans 3:23 says, we *all* have sinned and fallen short of the glory of God, owing a great debt we could never pay for on our own.

But in our hostile and indebted position, something happened to us, much like what happened to Edmund. Someone laid down His body of flesh in death, so that we might be reconciled back to the Father we were at odds with. But in our case, it wasn't a fictional lion from a fairy tale; it was the true and living Lion of Judah Himself, Jesus Christ. Like Edmund, because someone else decided to pay the price for our sin and bear our blame, now we are presented holy and blameless and above reproach.

Hear this loud and clear, friend: because of what Jesus has done for you through His death and resurrection, He has canceled the massive debt of sin that stood against you. He has eliminated every barrier that put you at odds with God. In Christ, you now stand before God as blameless, holy, and righteous. Not because of anything you did to earn it, but because of what Christ has accomplished for you on the cross. And you and I must stay rooted in the faith, remembering this to be our story. We must not forget such good news. We must cling to it. Just as Edmund could never forget what happened for him on that stone table, so should we never forget what has happened for us on the cross.

See, it is only through Christ—His sinless life, death on the cross to pay for our sin, and His resurrection—that we receive the forgiveness from God we could have never received on our own. There is nothing we can do or merit to ourselves in order to have the assurance of a saving faith. But in Christ and what He has done, we can have full assurance of our forgiveness before a holy God. We can now draw near to God with confidence because of Christ's sacrifice He made once for all (Heb. 10:10, 19–25). This is the glorious good news of the gospel.

But for the Colossians, the temptation is strong to forget this good news of the God who became man to die for the sins of sinners. Paul knows that surrounding heresy is sprouting up like weeds among the Colossians and reminds them to see the weeds for what they are in the beautiful garden God is sowing. He does not want them, or us, to be uprooted away from the gospel that they have already heard and received: the living hope of the good news of Jesus that has been announced to all creation under heaven. It's as if Paul is saying, "Don't forget! Remember what happened to you. Don't forget what Christ did to make you new. Don't let any other lie creep in and tell you otherwise! You've heard it proclaimed, you've received it as your own, you've held to it up till now. Don't shift from it in the days ahead! *This is who you are—reconciled and blameless.* All because of Christ."

So, what happens when we forget? What happens when we stumble and fall and need help to return to what's true? In 1 John 2:1, Jesus is described as our righteous advocate. The verse reads, "My little children, I am writing these things to you so that you may not sin. But if anyone does sin, we have an advocate with the Father, Jesus Christ the righteous." The passage doesn't say we *will* have an advocate; it says we have an advocate *already*. Did you know that Jesus is interceding right now for you? Do you know that He stands ready, right now, to help you and plead for you and advocate for you when you stumble and need His aid? Because He is righteous, He alone is able to intercede for you in this way and help you along. As Dane Ortlund puts it, "To come to the Father without an advocate is hopeless. To be allied with an advocate, one who came and sought me out rather than waiting for me to come to him, one who is righteous in all the ways I am not—this is calm and confidence before the Father."[1]

Friend, Jesus wasn't just your mediator before the Father on the cross; He's also your advocate right now. "He is able to save to the uttermost those who draw near to God through him, since he always lives to make intercession for them" (Heb. 7:25). He can help you when you forget. He can pick you back up when you stumble. He can forever defend your right to belong to the family of God, because He's the one who earned you entrance in the first place. When you struggle to remember the gospel for all the wonder that it is, go to your Advocate! He is your sure foundation and your safe place of refuge not just on the cross and in the resurrection, but right this very minute. He is your assurance and defense and confidence before the Father, even now. Praise God!

You can know without a doubt that God completely forgives those who have been justified by the body and blood of Christ. You can know with certainty and complete confidence that the sin you have committed, are currently battling against, and will ever commit in the future has been completely paid for by Jesus, to the uttermost. This is good news for the sinner, friend! And no false gospel or crooked message can undo it. Rest in the assurance you have in Christ, your advocate. Do not shift from it. Remember what He's done for you. Remember who you are. Reconciled instead of alienated. Blameless instead of guilty. Defended instead of abandoned. Advocated for instead of condemned. What other message could you possibly run to? What other news is better than this? None! Hold firm to the gospel, friend. It's truly the best news in the world.

RESPOND

1 / What other "messages" in your life compete with the gospel's message? Why are those messages so tempting sometimes?

2 / In your own words, what does it mean to be justified? How are we justified through Christ?

3 / Who in your life is still alienated from God and His people, or hostile in their minds? In what direction did Jesus run for these kinds of people—toward them, or away? Can you think of any examples in Scripture that help you answer that question of how Jesus responded to sinners? How does Jesus's example inform the steps you should take toward those who are far from God, or hostile in mind, this week?

4 / What did today's passage teach you about God's character? How can you live in response to this part of His character? Because God is

_____, I will _____.

PRAY

Heavenly Father, I thank You that although I was once alienated from You, hostile in mind and pursuing my own sinful desires, I am now reconciled to You through Your one and only Son. I thank You that by Christ's death and resurrection, I am justified before You. On the other side of grace, I am now blameless. No longer indebted. Advocated for. Defended and helped. No merit or good deeds could ever grant me such things, so I thank You and worship You right now for Your great kindness. I know other messages in this world compete against the good news of the gospel. I confess to You right now the messages I've been listening to, and I ask that You remind me of the truth. Guard me and give me greater wisdom and discernment to determine heresy or false teaching when I come across it—for there's no news like the gospel! I pray this in Jesus's precious name, amen.

Read Jeremiah 31:31–34.

Although written hundreds of years before Christ would come, the prophet Jeremiah is an advocate for the Israelites before God, pleading and praying for the forgiveness of his people who have sinned against God and turned to worthless idols and false gods. Jeremiah then forecasts the good news of the new covenant God's people would have one day in Christ.

What promise does Jeremiah give at the end of this passage that points us to the finished work of Christ, giving those who have trusted in Jesus full assurance of their faith in Him and forgiveness from God?

Why is Jesus an even better advocate for us compared to prophets like Jeremiah?

UNIFIED IN THE GOSPEL

READ / *Now I rejoice in my sufferings for your sake, and in my flesh I am filling up what is lacking in Christ's afflictions for the sake of his body, that is, the church, of which I became a minister according to the stewardship from God that was given to me for you, to make the word of God fully known, the mystery hidden for ages and generations but now revealed to his saints. To them God chose to make known how great among the Gentiles are the riches of the glory of this mystery, which is Christ in you, the hope of glory. Him we proclaim, warning everyone and teaching everyone with all wisdom, that we may present everyone mature in Christ. For this I toil, struggling with all his energy that he powerfully works within me.*

For I want you to know how great a struggle I have for you and for those at Laodicea and for all who have not seen me face to face, that their hearts may be encouraged, being knit together in love, to reach all the riches of full assurance of understanding and the knowledge of God's mystery, which is Christ, in whom are hidden all the treasures of wisdom and knowledge. I say this in order that no one may delude you with plausible arguments. For though I am absent in body, yet I am with you in spirit, rejoicing to see your good order and the firmness of your faith in Christ.

—Colossians 1:24–2:5

REFLECT / Have you ever longed to be reunited with someone you haven't seen in a long time? If you remember the start of the COVID-19 pandemic, your answer is probably yes. Remember when the whole world seemed to shut down? When our country entered a lockdown, we were urged to stay home, be away from other people including family that didn't live with us, and only take minimal trips to stores for essential items. Restaurants were closed, stores were closed, coffee shops were closed, even churches were closed. If you had asked any of us about an event like this, we would have thought it far-fetched or completely surreal. And yet we've lived through it. Total isolation. Separation from so many people we loved. And with that, a forgetfulness of our old rhythms.

If there's one thing I've grown to appreciate more since the pandemic, it is my local church. I now realize just how important it is to physically gather with my church family—something that just can't be replicated or replaced on a digital screen. It makes sense that we need church community (and relational connection with our broader community, too). After all, our triune God—Father, Son, and Spirit—is relational. And He made us in His image!

The church—the family of God. The gathering of the saints.. What a gift! A gift Paul knows well. In today's passage, we can clearly see just how vital a role the local church plays in the life of a Christian according to Paul. He can't stop mentioning the church. First, he says, in essence, that he's glad *he's* the one in the position of suffering instead of them (Col. 1:24). In this way, we can tell he longs for the church's well-being. Next, Paul calls the church Christ's "body," clearly showing us that he believes the local church is an extension of Christ Himself—His hands and feet in the world (Col. 1:24). Then, Paul tells us the church is not something that belongs to himself but is rather something God called Paul to *steward* (Col. 1:25). He became a minister of the church because God commissioned him to do so. The church, for Paul, isn't a group of people to entertain or to lord over; it's a gathering to steward and shepherd under God's permission, call, and delegation. The church is *God's*, not Paul's, and because it's God's, it should be valued and stewarded well not just by Paul but by all of us. Last, Paul says the church is supposed to experience something important—the preaching of God's "mystery," which is Christ (Col. 1:27).

How interesting. These Christians have already been told the mystery of Christ's gospel. They are already in Christ. So, what is Paul saying? He's saying we need to remember. He's saying that the church needs to *continually* hear the gospel's message, even though they've already heard it, and the amazing power it has in the life of the Christian. We forget it!

This reminds me of the story of the Israelites in the Old Testament. They are God's chosen people who have experienced all sorts of miraculous provision and intervention from God. They were rescued out of slavery in Egypt; they experienced firsthand God parting the Red Sea with Moses leading the way; they emerged on the other side of the waters unharmed. And yet how quickly they forgot who rescued them. And further in the story they continue to forget. As they journey through the wilderness, we watch how easily they forgot the One who provided for them and led them not just through the wilderness but into the promised land.

This theme of forgetfulness from God's chosen people comes up over and over again as you read the Old Testament. They repeatedly want to go back to their "comfort" in Egypt. And yet God, in His kindness and faithfulness to them, keeps on reminding and showing them who He is and what He *has* done for them—and what He *will* do for them.

We are so much like the Israelites. We have a need to remember, too. We so easily forget who God is, forget His character, forget His promises, forget what He *has* done for us through His Son and what He *will* do through His Son when He returns again (Mark 13:24–27; Col. 3:4; Heb. 9:28; Rev. 1:7). For Paul, one of the reasons the church should bask in the gospel every Sunday, week after week after week, is to *remember*. He wants them to remember their own story. He wants them to know they have been given a rich inheritance in Christ. He wants them to explore the depths of the glorious riches found in the gospel, which cannot be explored in one sitting or in just our moment of conversion. He doesn't want them to grow *beyond* the gospel, rather, *deeper into it* as they remember Christ and learn more about Him.

Paul loves the church and longs to gather with its people. He longs to preach the mysteries of the gospel to the people of God, helping them remember instead of forgetting. And he wants to fulfill his ministry with his dear Colossian brothers and sisters by his side.

But remember, Paul hasn't even met these Christians in Colossae yet. As we see in the rest of the passage today, he can't do all the things he longs to do with the church right now. For now, he's absent from their midst, which is difficult for him, as he deeply cares "for all who have not seen me face to face" (Col. 2:1). He might not have been facing the isolation of the COVID-19 pandemic, but he knew the sting of isolation while in prison. He longs to be reunited with the family of God.

As I mentioned before, I can relate to Paul's longing to physically be with these believers. I can remember the sting of feeling so isolated while we were physically separated from the body of Christ at my local church. Can you relate to Paul? If it wasn't the pandemic for you, can you think of a time when you felt all alone? And when you thought of gathering again with people, was the group you longed to gather with again the *church*? Or asked another way: If you were stuck in prison, would your first letter be to your church? Would they be the people you daydreamed about hanging out with again? I don't know about you, but that's convicting for me.

Friend, we are meant to do life together. Christians are especially meant to do life together. Discipleship can happen many ways—online Bible studies, college ministries, fun fellowship gatherings, and so on. But discipleship was meant to happen *primarily* through the local church. God created the church for His glory, for our good, and because of that, He commands us to be active members of His church. To do life together as God's family. More than a command, it should be a *longing* for us as it was for Paul.

And you know what happens when we prioritize the church at this level? We get to hear the gospel preached consistently to our hearts, and eventually, we get to make good on why Paul labored so hard, answering his prayers—meaning, we will eventually grow into mature Christians. That was his whole goal in ministry. That we'd mature into Christlikeness, not being deluded or deceived by other false cultural messages that swirl all around us (Col. 2:4). When we prioritize our local (and healthy) church, these things eventually become true about us. We will hear the gospel message so much and lock arms with other believers so often that we'll know *immediately* when another message has crept in to mislead us (or anyone else in our ranks).

Say this with me: "I need my Christian brothers and sisters." It's true! We need one another to be reminded of God's truth and the hope that we have in Christ when the world around us tries to pull up our anchor in Jesus and drift us away from Him. We need to be reminded of God's sovereignty. We need to be comforted by His people, who operate as His arms wrapping around us in hard times. We need help to remember Jesus is everything He says He is, as we learned yesterday: the Creator of all things, Sustainer of all things, and Reconciler of all things. We need our church family to tell us that nothing is outside of His control and that we can trust Him no matter our circumstances. As we lean into one another for these things, we get closer to a complete understanding and knowledge of our God. And over time we'll eventually find that we need not look to the things of this world to find true wisdom, knowledge, comfort, peace, or joy, for we have all these things and more in Christ, God's Word, and His family He's graciously given us!

Friend, do you have a church like this? Paul longs for churches to be this way, filled with God's Spirit and God's people, standing on God's Word, and basking in the mysterious riches of God's Son. If you don't have a church like this, find one! Isolation won't work long term for the Christian, and God longs for you to gather into the love and help of His people. I'm praying this for you if you don't have a church family like this yet and praising God with you if you do, friend.

RESPOND

1 / If you had to summarize the whole point of Paul's ministry, what would you say?

2 / What has your experience with the local church been? What gifts to the church might you need to offer? What fears might you need to overcome?

3 / In what ways do you need brothers and sisters in your church family right now? How can you reach out for help? On the flip side, who in your church community needs *you* right now? How can you minister to that person this week?

4 / In your own words, what does Paul say about suffering in Colossians 1:24? Based on this, does living the Christian life mean we will live a life free from suffering and trials? What are some practical things we can do when we face trials and suffering?

5 / What have you learned about God's character today? How can you live in response to this part of his character? Because God is

_____, I will _____.

PRAY

God, I thank You for loving Your church so much and for making me part of it. Thank You for people like Paul who have cared for the body of Christ, even when he was physically separated from them or hadn't even met them yet. I pray that You will reveal to me any ways I am isolating from the church—your body—and that You will give me the courage to step toward it with fresh faith. I pray that my local church will continue to be the things You've called us to be for one another—encouraging, challenging, rebuking, helping, comforting, and spurring one another on to continue toward maturity in Christ. I pray not only for my local church but also for Your global church. I pray that Your church in all of the world will be unified in the gospel and that You will guard it against the schemes of the enemy who continually tries to deceive the world with false ideas and teaching. Help us to be knitted together in love for you, Jesus. And give me fresh longing to come alongside my brothers and sisters who need my presence in their life right now. In Jesus's name, amen.

EXPLORE MORE

Read Genesis 2:18. Why do you think God says it is "not good" for the man to be alone? Was God not good enough for Adam, or was Adam's being alone not good enough for God? Use Genesis 1:26 to explain your answer below.

Read Romans 12:4–5. What does Paul say here about the church? Why does this matter in terms of gathering together with other believers regularly?

Read 1 Corinthians 14:26. What does Paul say here about good order in worship, and what happens when people from every tribe, nation, and tongue come together in corporate worship?

Read Hebrews 10:19–25. What does the author have to say about meeting together with our brothers and sisters in Christ? What reasons or benefits does the author give for why we should not neglect to meet together?

Read 1 Corinthians 11:17-25. What does Paul say is one of the primary reasons why believers should partake in the Lord's Supper in his letter he writes to the Corinthians? Is the taking of communion about us?

ROOTED AND BUILT UP IN HIM

READ / *Therefore, as you received Christ Jesus the Lord, so walk in him, rooted and built up in him and established in the faith, just as you were taught, abounding in thanksgiving.*

—Colossians 2:6–7

REFLECT / Roots. An essential part of any plant, the roots are the conveyor belt that gives water and nourishment to all the rest of the plant. Without a good root system, a plant can't survive. We can also think about the root being the basic cause, source, or initial origin of something—it's foundation. In both of these ways, Paul wants to remind us that Jesus is not just highest and best in our life, up at the top of our priority list, but He's also at the bottom too, holding up our whole life. He's the life source and the foundation on which everything else in our life is built. He sustains all things (Col. 1:17).

But Paul doesn't just point to Jesus as our root system or foundation; he also points to Jesus as the mold of what we're being built into. Think of it like a statue. A statue must be built on a firm foundation, or else it will crumble. For the Christian, that foundation is Christ. He is not just *a* foundation; He is *the* foundation! As 1 Corinthians 3:11 says, "For no one can lay a foundation other than that which is laid, which is Jesus Christ." We will crumble if our life isn't built on Him. And yet at the same time, the statue itself is also reliant on Jesus Christ, for *He's* the mold we're being shaped into. We aren't just being built into any old mold or building. No. As God builds on top of our foundation, we're being sculpted into a certain figure: Jesus Christ. We are slowly being shaped into *His* likeness.

But how do we go from just having a foundation to being built up into the sculpture, or likeness, of Christ? Paul makes it clear: what gets you from A to B is first *receiving* Christ to then *walking* in Him. Paul is sure these Colossian Christians have already heard and received the gospel (Col. 1:21–23), and now he encourages and commands these believers to continue walking obediently in Christ—and the same thing goes for you and me!

I love how *The Message* paraphrases it, making the connection super clear: "My counsel for you is simple and straightforward: Just go ahead with what you've been given. You received Christ Jesus, the Master; now *live* him. You're deeply rooted in him. You're well-constructed upon him. You know your way around the faith. Now do what you've been taught. School's out; quit studying the subject and start *living* it! And let your living spill over into thanksgiving."[2]

If I had to guess, you'd probably say Jesus Christ is your sure footing in this life. And I would too! If you've received Jesus Christ as your Lord and Savior, you've got a great foundation—the best! But what about *walking* in Him? If that's how we go from simply having a good foundation to becoming a beautiful statue, we must ask ourselves if we're actually walking like Jesus walked. As 1 John 2:6 reminds us, "Whoever says he abides in [Christ] ought to walk in the same way in which he walked."

Sister, I'm not sure what in your life right now is creating roadblocks and causing you to lose sight of your Savior and Source, Jesus. But I do know we *all*—every single one of us—can come up with some convincing rationale for receiving Christ without actually walking in line with His ways. Just as Paul reminds the Colossians to continue walking in the hope they have in Christ, this is something we need to be continually reminded of, too! Otherwise, we won't be built up into the likeness of Christ that we were meant to be sculpted into. We'll be left with a bare foundation—nothing built on top. And that won't do, for the whole purpose of a foundation is for something to be built on it!

What is holding you back from walking according to Christ? What is preventing you from building on the foundation you have in Him? What other likeness or "sculpture" are you being formed into, if not Christ's likeness? Whether it's sin that needs to be repented of, worldly distractions fighting for your attention and affection, a false gospel or false view of who God is that needs to be confronted, or deep grief or suffering you're walking through that perhaps is valid but is turning your heart *away* from God instead of *toward* Him, know that walking according to Christ is always the right way forward. He alone is where our hope is found. He is our sure foundation, the one we are to stay rooted in, be built up in, and sculpted into. May your heart be full of overflowing gratitude today for the hope you have received in Christ, and may you continue to walk in Him obediently. He is always the right way forward.

RESPOND

1 / Apart from Christ, what other foundations are you sometimes tempted to build your life on? Why?

2 / In what ways, or areas of life, are you not walking according to Christ's example? In these areas, if you aren't walking in Christ's ways, what or whose ways are you walking in?

3 / You likely already know you should walk according to Christ in the areas discussed in the last question. What specific roadblocks are hindering you from doing this? List them here and take time throughout the week to pray through this list, repenting when necessary, and asking God for wisdom and discernment as you seek to walk in obedience to Him.

4 / What does today's passage teach you about God's character, and how can you live in light of this? Because God is _____, I will _____.

PRAY

Thank You, Father, that You have chosen me to receive Christ! I am so grateful to have Him as my foundation, source, and hope. Nothing in this world could compare to such a gift. Help me move beyond just receiving Him to walking in Him. Build me up into His likeness. Help me walk obediently with You, and establish me in my faith as I walk according to the ways of Your Son. Reveal any roadblocks that are hindering me from walking like Jesus, and give me the courage to repent and take steps in the right direction, both for my good and for Your glory. Thank You for Your commitment to continually build me up in Christ, and thank You for giving Christ as my ever-present reason for overflowing gratitude. In Jesus's name, amen.

EXPLORE MORE

What does Jesus teach us about being rooted as we see Him teach the parable of the sower and the seed in Matthew 13:1–23? What are the different ways a person can be rooted? What is the best way to be rooted?

Read Matthew 7:24–27. What does it say about a firm foundation? A firm foundation and a solid house built upon it rely not just on receiving or hearing Jesus's words but what else (v. 24)? How does this teaching of Jesus in Matthew relate to what you've learned from Paul in Colossians 2:6–7?

RAISED WITH HIM

READ / *See to it that no one takes you captive by philosophy and empty deceit, according to human tradition, according to the elemental spirits of the world, and not according to Christ. For in him the whole fullness of deity dwells bodily, and you have been filled in him, who is the head of all rule and authority. In him also you were circumcised with a circumcision made without hands, by putting off the body of the flesh, by the circumcision of Christ, having been buried with him in baptism, in which you were also raised with him through faith in the powerful working of God, who raised him from the dead.*

—Colossians 2:8–12

REFLECT / I love the changing of the seasons we get to experience here in Minnesota. Living in a rural part of the state has given me a new appreciation for each season God has made for us to enjoy freely. Enjoying Minnesota summers and our many lakes is hard to beat, but fall, especially around our home, is probably my favorite time of the year. The changing of the leaves, the harvesting of the garden and prepping it for winter's rest, the busyness of summer coming to a lull until next year, the tradition of hunting my husband and our family enjoy, and the back-to-school routine I crave as summer comes to a close are all parts of autumn I look forward to each year. As for winter, there is so much beauty in the glittering snow as the sun shines down on it, in the frost-covered surfaces of the trees, and in every nook and cranny the morning fog nestles into. It truly is beautiful to take in, even on the sub-zero days. If you get outside and find ways to enjoy the winters here in Minnesota, it's really not so bad. Until about March and April . . . then the wintery days get a bit tiring as you feel spring inching closer. We've even seen snow in May though, and that's when it's really not okay anymore for the flakes to fly!

But when that glorious spring season finally comes, it truly is like a breath of fresh air. It's like being underwater and coming up for that big breath (or in the days of a pandemic, getting to finally take your mask off after running to the grocery store!). Seeing new life burst forth out of the dead of winter reminds me of the beautiful reality of the resurrection for those who have trusted in Jesus.

In today's passage we see the beauty of the newness in Christ we have. As Paul reminds the Colossians, they (and we!) have "been buried with him in baptism, in which you were also raised with him through faith in the powerful working of God, who raised him from the dead" (Col. 2:12).

This is the good news of the gospel—a life-giving spring that flies in the face of a terrible winter. Jesus—the perfect, sinless, spotless Lamb—died for the sins of all mankind. He took our place. He bore our iniquities. He died the death we deserve. He willingly went to the cross in order to save us. But that wasn't the end of the story. Our sin, our shame, our past, and our condemnation from a holy God isn't the end of our story, either. In Jesus we are no longer slaves to our sin or held captive by "philosophy and empty deceit," meaning that we no longer have to be led around on a leash by the deceptive, earthly wisdom of this world.

And more than just being free from this captivity here and now, we are promised resurrection life on the other side of death. Just as Jesus was buried and then raised to life, all those who have trusted in Christ have the assurance that we will be raised to life with Him, too. That's right—just as Jesus walked out of His grave, you will walk out of yours too one day, in a glorified body that is built to live in the new heavens and earth *forever* (Phil. 3:20–21). I don't know what empty deceit or false philosophies of this world are swirling around you today, but none of them can give you *that* kind of future! Resurrection life can only come through Christ (John 11:25). This is why He's highest and best. He's the only one who can fully pay for sin, defeat death, and offer *real* hope for believers on the other side of this world's story.

As we've touched on previously, that's one of Paul's main concerns for this young church. He doesn't want them to be led astray by false gospels, deceptive ways of thinking, or earthly promises that can't actually deliver the way Jesus can. These false promises make their way into churches all the time, and the Colossian church is no different. It faced the same risks as any church today does. In the face of this, Paul wants these believers to hold fast to the only payment of sin that justifies them before a holy God, who is Christ Himself, that now declares them forgiven, sin completely paid for now, forever and always. Paul is reminding them, and us, that in Christ, they have died to their old self, or as he puts it in today's passage, "putting off the body of the flesh." They have walked away from those false ways of thinking. They have given up on worldly wisdom. They have found the true way to find life in Jesus, and after going down into the waters of baptism, they were symbolically "raised up" to new life out of the waters, a practice which points to the new life we have in Christ as believers but also the future we have in the resurrection when we'll all be raised up forever. In all these ways and more, these Colossians have hitched their wagon to Christ, and Paul doesn't want them going back to the elementary ways of the world that they once clung to before Him.

What elementary ways of the world did you cling to before you hitched your wagon to Jesus? What kind of spiritually immature, earthly thinking held you captive? What kind of false messages swirl around you right now? Remember the truth, friend: as followers of Christ, our former self and ways of living have been buried with Christ, our hearts have been raised to new life, and our bodies will be raised to new life eternally as well in the resurrection. For the Christian, this good news is our greatest hope as we live today and even as we face death. In life and in death, our assurance and confidence spring eternal because Christ is our hope! Let us live today and all of our days in light of this truth, and be on guard, alert for any other lie that might come against it. There's no message like the gospel's message—no greater freedom and no greater future that could ever be promised to us. Remember and rest in Jesus, friend. And then go out and proclaim this amazing good news to the people around you! Everyone needs Jesus. Give them the best news ever! Give them Jesus.

RESPOND

1 / In our passage for today in Colossians 2, Paul says this about Jesus: "For in him the whole fullness of deity dwells bodily." Back in Colossians 1, Paul said something similar: "For in him all the fullness of God was pleased to dwell" (v. 19). In your own words, when you consider both these verses, what is Paul's big point? Why do you think he repeats this idea for us? Why is it so significant for us to understand?

2 / Reread Colossians 2:8. This is not the first time Paul has brought up his big concern with the church in Colossae. He seems to bring it up often throughout his letter. What is his main concern for them? Why is this important?

3 / Think back to chapters 1 and 2. Paul has gone to great lengths to show us the sufficiency and centrality of Christ. In this passage we see a contrast. Paul makes a point to prove the deficiency of something compared to Christ. What is it?

4 / List some common idols of our world and the promises these idols make us. In what ways do these pale in comparison to the hope we have in Christ and the future we have in the resurrection?

5 / What did today's passage teach you about God's character, and how can you live in light of this? Because God is _____, I will _____.

Thank You, God, that life with Your Son Jesus gives me an eternal spring in the harshest of winters! Thank You that because Jesus was buried and raised to life, I will be raised to new life too! Thank You, God, that in a world of lies, You've given me the truth in Jesus. I ask that You would guard me against empty deceit and philosophies of this world that will only prove to be deficient compared to the surpassing worth and sufficiency of Christ. Give me wisdom to know false teaching when I hear or see it, and do not let me stray back into the old, immature, elementary ways of thinking in my former days. I do not want to go back to the ways of the world or the habits of my old self, for Your gospel gives me a better and brighter future. Help me stay anchored in You, and help me teach those around me to do the same.

EXPLORE MORE

Read 2 Corinthians 5:17. What does Paul mean when he says, "Therefore, if anyone is in Christ, he is a new creation"?

In this passage, we learned that baptism is a sign that we are part of God's family and united to Christ as we go down into the water and then are raised up, signifying new life in Jesus. Read Matthew 28:16–20 and Titus 3:1–11 and make note of what you find out in these two passages that talk about baptism. What new insights have you gained? Make note of those too, and thank God for revealing that to you!

Finally, to prepare for tomorrow's reading, let's consider what the Scriptures say about circumcision and uncircumcision. As you explore what Moses (in Genesis) and Paul (in Galatians) have to say about the matter, take some notes on how each of these verses helps set the stage for what Colossians might want to "get at" in tomorrow's reading.

Genesis 17
Galatians 5:2–6

MADE ALIVE

READ / *And you, who were dead in your trespasses and the uncir-cumcision of your flesh, God made alive together with him, having forgiven us all our trespasses, by canceling the record of debt that stood against us with its legal demands. This he set aside, nailing it to the cross. He disarmed the rulers and authorities and put them to open shame, by triumphing over them in him.*

—*Colossians 2:13–15*

REFLECT / What's your favorite epic story? It could be a book or even a movie. Whether it's a film built for movie critics or little kids, chances are, death and life are big themes—and I bet there's a climactic scene where life triumphs over death. Think about it. What's the most heart-tugging scene in *Beauty in the Beast*? When the Beast dies but rises up in rays of glory, alive, due to true love. What's the most suspenseful moment in *Harry Potter*? When Harry dies but is brought back to the land of the living through the power of the resurrection stone. What's the jaw-dropping scene in The Chronicles of Narnia? When Aslan is killed on the stone table but then comes roaring back to life with the sun beaming behind him and an authoritative growl so intense that his enemies must've heard it and run for the hills! Life on the other side of death is the strongest story humans know how to tell.

The same is true when it comes to the central message of Christianity. In fact, if you were looking for a passage in Scripture that describes the heart of the Christian faith, you can find it here, tucked in the middle of the book of Colossians. As we look closer at this portion of Scripture, we first see who we were before accepting Christ as our Savior: dead. We were dead in our sin, living for the passions of our flesh. Not "sick." Not "barely breathing." Not "in need of improvement." *Dead*. We were the Beast, immovable and limp on the ground. Harry, out cold on the forest floor. Aslan, bound and lifeless on the cracked stone.

In stark contrast, we then see the other side of the story. Because of our justification in Christ, we are now *alive*. We are a brand-new creation in Christ. *God made us alive with Him in Christ* (Col. 2:13). Instead of limp and lifeless, we rise on our feet, roaring with faith and vitality in Jesus. What an amazing truth for the Christian!

But there was a cost for such a gift. Jesus paid the price to give us new life, canceling our debt that stood against us that we could never repay, nailing our sin onto the Man of Sorrows who hung on the cross, in agony, separated from the Father for our sake. "For our sake [God the Father] made [Christ] to be sin who knew no sin, so that in him we might become the righteousness of God" (2 Cor. 5:21). And this wasn't just the Father's doing. The Son volunteered to do it. He laid His life down of His own volition, all for true love of us (John 10:17–18). The Spirit, too, agreed on the mission and empowered it. Notice the verse doesn't just say Jesus made you alive. Rather, *God* made you alive—God who is triune: God the Father, God the Son, and God the Holy Spirit, all involved in the salvation project to bring you back from the dead into the land of the living! This is very good news.

Made alive in Christ. Thank you, Lord! Our old, botched-up track record nailed to the cross for good. Hallelujah! You'd think the good news would stop right there, but if we keep reading, we see it doesn't. If we keep reading, we see that the work of Jesus on the cross not only affects us, but it also affects another party—the "rulers and authorities," as Paul talks about them. And who are they, exactly? Paul answers this question clearly in his letter to the Ephesians: they are the "rulers" and "authorities" and "cosmic powers" that reign "over this present darkness"—or in short, "the spiritual forces of evil in the heavenly places" (Eph. 6:12). In other words, Paul is referencing Satan and his "minions," if you will, who have roamed in the spiritual realm and attacked the people of God. He says that now, because of Jesus's blood shed on the cross and His body raised in the resurrection, evil is now "disarmed" and "put to open shame."

Do you see the contrast here? The people of God are made alive and given new identities to walk in. With a sinful record now nailed to the cross, we get fellowship with God! The enemies of God, on the other hand, are stripped down and disgraced in front of the whole host of heaven. Without a record to accuse us—after all, that old record has been paid for and cancelled by Christ!—they have no power over us anymore. Instead of shaming us for our past deeds, now they are the ones who receive open shame. As Romans 8:1 says, "There is therefore now *no* condemnation for those who are in Christ Jesus" (emphasis added). With your record being nailed to the cross, Satan doesn't have a case in the courtroom of heaven! With the true Ruler of the universe, Jesus, sitting on His rightful throne, all the lesser authorities and rulers are sent packing. They may have tried to rule before Jesus resurrected, but now He proves that His lordship extends not only over you but over *them*. Amazing!

In Christ, friend, you get *life*. You get fellowship. You get a rap sheet that's paid for and fully canceled. And your ultimate spiritual enemy gets stripped down and sent packing. Death is dead. Christ is risen. We now rejoice in His victory. It was completely finished upon the cross!

Only Jesus can do this. Only Jesus can triumph over every single thing that could keep us from being made alive together with God. Only Jesus can bring us from death to life. Only Jesus can disarm the enemy, who once accused us before God in the heavenly realm, proving his case that we couldn't obey the law and that we were in the wrong. The enemy may have been right at one time about that, but because Jesus lived the life we should have lived and died the death we deserved, he isn't anymore! That record Satan used to accuse us is now long gone. Handled. Paid in full. And now we're declared *right* before God instead of wrong. Only Jesus, friend. Only Jesus.

Doesn't that make you see Him as highest and best? Doesn't that make you want to put Him first? After all, there's no other Savior like this. Whether or not you want to put Him first, highest, and best, the truth is that *He is*. Because He's the one who has made you alive. He is the one who has brought you near. He is the one who has disarmed your enemy.

So today, remember your newness in life. Remember your sins have been completely paid for at the highest cost by the triumphant Savior of the world. Remember that your enemy is the one who stands in open shame before heaven now, not you. Sin and death no longer have the final say in your story. Walk in obedience to Him today knowing that there is no greater part of your story than this.

RESPOND

1 / Remember your own story with Jesus. What sins were you dead in before God brought you to life in Christ? What sorts of things in your life did God nail to the cross? Take some time to thank God for this.

2 / What new insights from Colossians 2 help you put Jesus first in your life?

3 / How does it make you feel to know that God the Father, God the Son, and God the Spirit wanted to make new life possible for you? What does this teach you about the character of God?

4 / We learned today that the gospel's news of Jesus's lordship not only applies to humans but to all spiritual realms, too. Why is this significant? How does it change the way you live?

5 / How can you live in light of God's character, as discovered in this passage? Because God is _____, I will _____.

PRAY

Heavenly Father, thank You that in Your great grace, You took me from death to life! Thank You for saving me through Your one and only Son. And Jesus, thank You for laying your life down voluntarily on the cross so that all my sins would be nailed to it, paid for in full, once and for all. Thank You for loving me enough to offer me such a gift. I praise You, Jesus, for proving Yourself not just my Lord, but Lord over all, including the spiritual forces in the world around me. You are Lord over all—the seen and unseen, over everything I can't even fully understand, even spiritual forces of evil in the heavenly places. You are sovereign and infinite, God. I praise You for who You are! You have proven Yourself the victor over all authorities and rulers in the spiritual realm, and You have taken away their ability to accuse me, which gives me great hope and confidence. Help me live in light of this truth today, and reveal any sin that might be preventing me from intimacy with You. Help me triumph over my struggles with sin in the power of Your Spirit, help me put You first in everything, and help me become more like You as I walk according to Your ways. Amen.

Read Luke 7:36–50. Explain how this beautiful story of Jesus forgiving a sinful woman relates to our Scripture today when Paul reminds the Colossians that they were once dead in their trespasses but now have been made alive together with God and completely forgiven of the debt that stood against us.

Read Hebrews 2:14 and compare it to Colossians 2:15. How do the two passages shed light on each other? In what ways does this help you consider Jesus highest and best, Lord above all lords, and King above all kings?

Read Ephesians 6:10–18. List all the things Paul describes as the "armor of God." What "armor" do you dress yourself well with daily? What armor do you need to remember to put on more often daily? What does that say about the character of God that He gives His people the defense we need against Satan and the spiritual forces of evil in the heavenly realms?

JESUS IS THE SUBSTANCE

READ / *Therefore let no one pass judgment on you in questions of food and drink, or with regard to a festival or a new moon or a Sabbath. These are a shadow of the things to come, but the substance belongs to Christ. Let no one disqualify you, insisting on asceticism and worship of angels, going on in detail about visions, puffed up without reason by his sensuous mind, and not holding fast to the Head, from whom the whole body, nourished and knit together through its joints and ligaments, grows with a growth that is from God.*

—Colossians 2:16–19

REFLECT / If you were a fly on the wall in our home, one of the frequent make-believe games you will find my kids playing is "coffee shop." In typical kid-like fashion, my ever-observant kids took an interest in "brewing" their own lattes at home and having "Sunshine Coffee Shop" open weekly as they have watched me familiarize myself with our new espresso machine. They watch carefully how the machine grinds the high-quality beans. How I pack down the ground espresso with the tamper. How I lock the filter in place and press the button so that hot water hits the grounds and becomes a shot of espresso. How I combine the shot with milk in a bunch of different ways to make all sorts of specialty coffee drinks, right from home!

While the coffee shop games are fun, one thing has been a bummer. With all this newfound learning about quality espresso drinks in my home, it's now hard for me to go to regular old coffee shops. I can now taste the difference between the real, high-quality thing and the fake stuff. I know, I know—I'm a coffee snob!

On top of the coffee itself, another aspect goes into our coffee shop game: the money it takes to pay for the coffee. Naturally, as the adult in the scenario, it's easy for me to tell the difference between real money and the pretend money my kids give me to pay for their "coffees." Wouldn't that be nice to be able to pay for things with white construction paper cut-outs of coins and dollar bills like the IKEA cash register we use when we play?

In all seriousness, though, here's what I've learned: taking time to appreciate knowing the "real thing," whatever that thing is, helps you know that the fake, is, well, . . . fake.

Think about it: how can I tell the difference between real and counterfeit money? I've spent a lot of time around real money. I have paid for gas with it, pulled it out of my wallet at restaurants, tipped the pizza guy with it, and so on. I know what it feels like and what it looks like because I've spent years handling it. The same goes for good coffee. The more time I spend around it—tasting it, making it, learning about it—the more I can detect the presence of really bad coffee!

Similarly, the Colossians have already heard and learned and received the true, real gospel (Col. 1:3–7). Paul's hope is that these Colossians will keep holding on to this true gospel instead of drinking down fake versions of it. His words spur them on to remember the truth and the substance of their faith, who is Christ, in the face of false teaching.

But what sort of false teaching? The answer is not made completely clear to us in this letter, but we are given some clues as we read about parts of the issue that was going on. Ultimately, given how much ink Paul spills on the sufficiency of Christ, it's clear that false teachers were trying to add in other things that one must do to be assured of their salvation in addition to the complete and finished work of Christ. For example, the Jewish diet and calendar observances (food and drink, new moon sacrifices, festivals, Sabbaths, etc.). Apparently, some false teachers were teaching that these Jewish observances were a "must" for believers to practice in order to be a real Christian.

But Paul wouldn't have that! While these Jewish practices had their place, the big point is that they were a foreshadowing of Christ, who had already come! When it comes to the Jewish festival of lights, for example, *Jesus is our light* (John 8:12). Or when it comes to the laundry list of rules surrounding the Sabbath in Jewish culture, *Jesus is our rest* (Matt. 11:28–30). Paul's main point is that simply *being in Christ* is sufficient. Why? Because while all those other practices are the shadow, Jesus is the object. The substance. The real thing. He is highest and best because He is the substance and the fulfillment of all those rituals that had come before Him. What was once foreshadowed has now been fulfilled! All those rituals were pointing to *Him*!

In other examples, some teachers were likely encouraging the worship of angels and ecstatic emotional experiences as necessary practices for Christian living, only possible if a worshipper deprives his body and treats it harshly (*asceticism*). The logic went like this: *if I deprive myself of enough, God will give me extraordinary spiritual experiences*. But as Paul will go on to say (as we will see in the passage we explore tomorrow), while these self-made religions and asceticism have an appearance of wisdom, they are actually "of no value in stopping the indulgence of the flesh" (Col. 2:23). In other words, all of these things don't actually change a person. They can't stop a person from sinning, they can't save a person, and they can't make a person live righteously because they aren't the true, real gospel. In stark opposition to Christ, they don't hold any substance. Next to Jesus, they are fake, and always will be!

And so, with all these false ideas running rampant in the church, Paul wants the Colossians, and us, to hear this loud and clear: *Jesus alone is sufficient* to supply what we need for our conversion and also the race we run in the faith after being saved. Nothing else needs to be added! No other experience or ritual is required.

Paul does not want this young church to drift away from this vital truth. He wants them to hold tight to the gospel of Jesus that they have already heard and received. He doesn't want them to add to the gospel, as if their works could fill in something lacking to Christ's work of atonement and resurrection. He wants them to rest in Jesus, who is the substance of all the things they need.

Friend, Christ alone holds the power to save sinners. He alone has what it takes to nourish and completely satisfy our weary souls. We are saved not by religious practices, extreme deprivation, or wild spiritual experiences but by grace alone through faith alone in Jesus Christ alone (Eph. 2:8–9). And here's the encouraging part: if you believe the true gospel, nothing and no one can disqualify you from the saving grace of Jesus Christ. This is good news! He who began a good work in the Colossians is the same Savior who has begun a good work in you, and He will bring it to completion when He returns again (Phil. 1:6).

Take this with you today: you don't need the shadow; you've got the real thing. Christ is first and highest, because He alone can save, sanctify, and satisfy you. May you rest in this hope today and always!

RESPOND

1 / In what ways do you try to add to Christ's work to gain favor with God? How does today's passage help free you from this?

2 / Why do false gospels or good works tend to puff us up? In other words, why do false gospels or good works make us prideful or give us false confidence before God?

3 / What new insights from today's devotional motivate you to put Jesus first in your life? What from today's passage has helped you see that He deserves to be highest and best in your heart?

4 / Think about things that might offer you temporary satisfaction in the world. List them out here, then bring those before God, and ask Him to remove these temporary satisfactions and replace them with the hope of the gospel.

5 / What does this passage teach you about God's character, and how can you live in light of that? Because God is _____, I will
_____.

Jesus, You are all I need! I am so often tempted, like the Colossians were, to add to the gospel's good news. I trust in Your finished work, but sometimes I try to tack things on in addition to it, as if this will gain me more favor with God. And yet doing so only undermines all You've done for me. I stand here before you today and confess the truth: what You've done is enough. Your sacrifice on the cross was not lacking! You are sufficient to save and to sustain me. You are highest and best! I repent of the things I often look to save me, comfort me, and fill me because only You are sufficient to do these things. Help me recognize when I try to rely on some other tactic to find favor with the Father, and give me wisdom and discernment to know if I'm being taught something that contradicts your gospel. In Your name, amen.

EXPLORE MORE

We are now at the halfway mark in our journey through Colossians. Congratulations, my friend!

Before we began this devotional together, I told you that periodically we would pause in our journey through Colossians to catch our breath and look at the map again, reorienting ourselves to the big picture so that we can keep moving forward in confidence. Today is that day. Let's stop for a moment and get a bird's-eye view of the map again. Sometime today I encourage you to engage in repeated reading again, a good Bible literacy practice (see "Bible Study Tips" in the back of the book for reference).

So here's what I want you to do: go back to day 1 of our devotional to recount the important questions we considered before we started the devotional: Who wrote it? How was it written? To whom was it written? When was it written? And why was it written? Make note of anything new you noticed, questions you had previously that are now clearer or have been answered, or questions you still have as you reread this letter through in one sitting.

Repeated reading reflections:

BETTER THAN RULES

READ / *If with Christ you died to the elemental spirits of the world, why, as if you were still alive in the world, do you submit to regulations—"Do not handle, Do not taste, Do not touch" (referring to things that all perish as they are used)—according to human precepts and teachings? These have indeed an appearance of wisdom in promoting self-made religion and asceticism and severity to the body, but they are of no value in stopping the indulgence of the flesh.*

—Colossians 2:20–23

REFLECT / I love rules, I love order. They make me feel safe and like I have my stuff together. I love checking things off in my planner or crumbling up and throwing away a Post-it note into the trash when I've completed the items I wrote out. These things make me feel accomplished. A funny thing I'll even do sometimes is write out everything I've already accomplished in my planner, just so I can cross it off. Have you done that before? Just me, the crazy, task-lister, one?

While rules are good and have their right place, unfortunately, sometimes my striving to keep rules and order doesn't always mean that my heart is in the right order. Instead of the sufficiency of Christ ruling in my heart, my own sinfulness—my pride, my self-ishness, my self-sufficiency—is what rules within me. My checklist may be accomplished, but there's still a lot of work to be done inside my heart.

Maybe you can relate. Maybe you know what this striving feels like. Striving for comfort and control. Striving to be sufficient enough on my own, apart from Christ.

Our passage for today probably feels a little bit familiar, and it should. It's sort of like "part 2" to the devotional from yesterday because it has similar themes. Yesterday we encountered some clues about the false teaching going on in the Colossian church—teaching that says Christians must add certain rules and regulations to their salvation in order to be saved. Here, Paul takes the logic a little bit further. His point is this, in essence: "Listen, you've put all your striving behind you when you came to Christ. You heard the gospel—the good news that told you Jesus did everything necessary to save you and sustain you. Why do you go back to striving, then? Why do you submit to a bunch of man-made rules when Christ has fulfilled all the rules in your place? *Don't touch this or don't taste that*—rules like this can't save you, even if you could keep them! Rest in Jesus, who fulfilled all the rules, and walk in freedom instead of putting on old chains!"

Do you feel like this message of Christ's sufficiency is getting a little . . . repetitive? Good! That's Paul's whole point. He *wants* to drone on about this. He needs these Colossians to get it. They will stray if they do not hear this over and over: Christ died on the cross so that sinners could be made right with God, and Christ alone holds the power to save the sinner. Nothing in this world, including rules and regulations, can replace what Christ has done to bring salvation and sustainment to God's people. They (and we!) are no longer slaves to their sin or to the law they could never keep perfectly because God sent His one and only Son to obey it perfectly in their place. *Don't try to do what Christ has already done for you, Paul pleads. Hold fast to Him!*

And there's more. Paul not only makes the point that these extra rules can't save the Colossians; he also makes clear that keeping the rules on the other side of salvation can't keep Christians from indulging in the flesh. What's his point? That although all these practices give off the *appearance* of being super-spiritual or pious, they are really all for show. They are just a veneer, a cover-up, and they have no real spiritual power to help you fight your flesh anyway. They look high and mighty, but they are void of power. Only God has the power you need to help you fight your sin and temptations.

Friend, rules won't make you less sinful. Rules won't save you. Rules won't make you desire the right things in the moments your heart desires all the wrong things. Rules might restrain you from some forms of evil, but *they can't change you from the inside out.* Only Christ is sufficient for that.

Jesus can change you, friend. And doesn't this truth make you want to put Him as highest and best in your life? No matter how strong the temptation to add to His work, remember what Paul is telling the Colossians: as a follower of Christ, you are not bound by human commands and doctrines. Following the rules won't cut it. If that were true, then you could rely on your own self-sufficiency. But even on your best self-reliant days, you will never do it perfectly. In our own strength we will never be enough. *And you don't have to be.* In Christ you have the freedom to let go of your unending striving and rest in His finished work displayed on the cross and the resurrection. When the world tries to tell you differently—to do life in the power of your own strength and striving—remember, you have been raised to new life in Christ. You've been made alive together with Him (Col. 2:13), and by His Spirit, you have the ability to walk righteously without being forced. Those rule-keeping chains are gone. You are no longer bound by empty rituals, as if those would grant you favor with God. You have Jesus. Through His reconciling work, you have favor with God already! And nothing can take Him away from you.

We are not enough, but Christ is. And that is good news, friend. Rest in this truth today.

RESPOND

1 / If you sense a need for change in your life, what tactics do you typically trust to change yourself? How have those tactics failed you in the past?

2 / In what areas of your life are you trying to claim all-sufficiency? In what ways do you need to acknowledge your lack and rest in the sufficiency of Christ?

3 / What new reason has this passage given you for considering Jesus as highest and best?

4 / What did today's passage teach you about God's character? How can you live in response to this part of His character today? Because God is _____, I will _____.

God, I thank You that I am not enough. What freedom is found in these words. My striving can cease when I remember that Your Son, Jesus, is sufficient for salvation and for sustainment! I confess to You right now that I have tried to rely on my own hard work to gain Your favor; You know the ways I've done this. I bring these failed attempts to You and ask that You help me rest in Christ, who obeyed all the rules in my place because He knew I never could. Help me change, not by the power of rules but by the power of Jesus. And help me become more and more like Him. In Jesus's name, amen.

EXPLORE MORE

Read Romans 8:29–39. What does Paul have to say here in his letter to the Romans about what separates us from the love of God for those who are in Christ Jesus?

Read Ephesians 2:4–10. According to this Scripture, how is a person saved? How are people not saved? Why is this good news for the sinner?

Read Matthew 5:17–20. What does Jesus say about the law in these verses? Why is Jesus alone able to fulfill the law?

THINK LIKE HEAVEN

READ / *If then you have been raised with Christ, seek the things that are above, where Christ is, seated at the right hand of God. Set your minds on things that are above, not on things that are on earth. For you have died, and your life is hidden with Christ in God. When Christ who is your life appears, then you also will appear with him in glory.*

—Colossians 3:1–4

REFLECT / Have you ever been reading your Bible, or accomplished a task you had been working on, or simply enjoyed a moment where you were feeling so content with where God has you in life and what He has given you . . . only to open up your social media app and suddenly all those feelings fly out the window?

Suddenly what you had just accomplished seems like nothing as you scroll and see what that other person achieved that day. Suddenly that feeling of contentment has vanished after seeing another person with her perfectly put-together home, filled with the latest and greatest—not to mention her perfect husband and kids in the background. Suddenly you feel overwhelmed and behind on everything. Joy in what God's allowed you to achieve that day is now replaced with anxiety to get more done. Contentment in your circumstances and gifts given by God are now replaced with discontentment and displeasure.

I've been there. It's like all the good gifts God has given me evaporate—like suddenly the blinders go on, and what's left in my view is everything I now think I need to have or do to be satisfied. My mind and eyes are set on earthly things instead of heavenly things. It's a terrible feeling!

It's easy to think that this is a modern problem, all due to social media. But that's just not true. Paul's words in today's passage show us that the Colossians, too, struggled with this problem. Apparently, it's an ancient one! And Paul doesn't want the problem to take over. He doesn't want the Colossians to lose their satisfaction in Christ. He doesn't want them to start looking to the left and to the right and lose sight of Jesus. And knowing the current threat of false teaching that is happening, Paul knows that losing sight of Jesus isn't just a "maybe thing." It's a real possibility for this church—and for you and me!

To cast their gaze in the right direction, Paul reminds the Colossians of some much-needed truth. He offers them the perspective they need—and that we need—to keep our eyes in the right place. First, he says we have been raised with Christ (Col. 3:1). Next, he makes clear exactly where Christ is: "seated at the right hand of God." What does this mean? It means that from God's perspective, if we are in Christ, our place is with Him in heaven, right beside Him (Eph. 2:4–6). We are as good as seated right next to Christ, who is right next to the Father. It's a sure thing, a done deal, from heaven's vantage point. From our perspective, given that we are time bound and still on the earth right now, we haven't gotten there yet. But because we're found in Christ, we may as well be!

This is incredible news for the Colossians and for us. This amazing truth reminds us of our identity. We are a citizen of heaven (Phil. 3:20), and in Christ, we are seated there already. Because we belong to Him, we belong in His realm.

Considering this, Paul's next command makes a lot of sense: "Set your minds on things that are above, not on things that are on earth" (Col. 3:2). Well, of course we should be thinking according to heaven—that's where we belong. That's where we are seated, from heaven's perspective, right next to Christ. We should be thinking with eternity in mind and living with eternity in mind, too. That's our home. While we wait to dwell with God in our forever home, we can rejoice now at this truth: we are seated with Christ and made alive through his death on the cross. We don't have to wait until we get to heaven to experience this. We can joyfully think and live out this beautiful reality, now! If God views us as basically already in the heavenly realm, why would we think according to the earthly realm? Why would our minds be stuck on the way the world does things? Why would we seek things of the earth?

And yet if we're honest, we *do* set our minds on the things on earth. We forget who we are. We forget *whose* we are. We forget what kingdom we truly belong to. The Colossians understand. Right now, false teaching is making its way into their church, which tempts them to keep their mind off the things above and instead fixate on worldly concerns. Paul urgently reminds them to fight this temptation. He urges them to keep their minds fixed on Jesus and not on things of this earth. He lifts their gaze to heaven and says, "If you're as good as up there, then think as if you're someone who, in fact, belongs up there! You have been raised with Christ to the heavenly places, so think that way. The things your mind is set on should be the things of heaven." And who is the biggest, most important "thing" in heaven? Jesus! He is our reward in heaven, whom we will never stop worshipping along with "a great multitude that no one could number, from every nation, from all tribes and peoples and languages, standing before the throne and before the Lamb" (Rev. 7:9–10).

As followers of Jesus, we are to seek knowing and loving Him above all things. We are to set our minds on Him, always keeping Him in focus when the enemy and the world around us seek to grab our attention and affections for earthly things and confuse where our true identity is found—in Christ.

Friend, your identity is secure in Christ, and so is your future. You don't need to fixate on anything this world has to offer, because Jesus is better. He is preeminent, raised up, highest, and best. Live and *think* like you believe that's true.

Glory will be your prize when He, who is your life, appears (Col. 3:4). When He comes back, you won't just be "as good as" with Him in heaven; you'll become like Him in glory, *actually* by His side as He is, resurrected and glorified. Until that glorious day, we can *think* like we believe it is coming. We can set our minds on that day and the Savior who will make it come to pass. And such thinking will help us walk in a manner worthy of Jesus here and now (Col. 1:10; 2:6) with full, unwavering hope in Him not because of anything we've done or accomplished, but because of everything He has already accomplished on our behalf in His life, death, and resurrection.

Friend, keep your heart and mind fixed on the all-sufficient founder and perfecter of our faith (Heb. 12:1–3). You have been raised with Him. You will be made fully like Him when He comes again. Don't look down on earthly distractions. Keep your eyes up.

RESPOND

1 / When Paul says not to focus on the things of earth, do you think he means that we should never think about the daily issues and concerns going on in this world—like our families, cultural issues, or the roles and responsibilities God has given us? If not, what do you think are the "things that are on earth" that Paul means? What kind of worldly concerns could he be talking about?

2 / What lesser things typically distract you from thinking about Jesus or heavenly concerns? How might you prepare for this distraction next time and fight the temptation to look away from Jesus? Asked another way, what specific practices will help you set your minds on the things of heaven?

3 / What questions do you have about the resurrection, when you will appear with Jesus as He is? Whom could you approach with these questions?

4 / What does today's passage teach you about God's character? How can you live in response to this part of His character today? Because God is _____, I will _____.

Father, thank You for not only raising up Christ but for raising me up with Him! Thank You for considering me as good as next to you! What grace You have shown me. I confess that I have not fixed my mind on the things of heaven, Your dwelling place, where Christ is seated. I easily get distracted by the things of earth. You know the specific ways I struggle here, and I bring them before You now. I pray You'll help me, by Your Holy Spirit, to set my mind on Jesus. Help me make a daily habit of putting Him first in every aspect of my life. Thank You that because of Him I will one day be with You in glory. It's in Jesus's mighty name I pray, amen.

EXPLORE MORE

Read Philippians 4:8–9. Write out the things Paul tells the Philippians to think on or "set their minds on." How can this list help you take all your thoughts captive before they spiral down to the what-ifs, made-up scenarios, or second-guessing?

Read Hebrews 12:1–3.

- *What does the author of Hebrews tell us to throw off that hinders us?*
- *What are we to do after that?*
- *Who are we to look to always?*
- *What, or who, was Jesus's joy that was set before Him when He endured the cross? Where is Jesus now?*
- *Why is this good news for you?*

THROW OFF THE
OLD CLOTHES!

READ / *Put to death therefore what is earthly in you: sexual immorality, impurity, passion, evil desire, and covetousness, which is idolatry. On account of these the wrath of God is coming. In these you too once walked, when you were living in them. But now you must put them all away: anger, wrath, malice, slander, and obscene talk from your mouth. Do not lie to one another, seeing that you have put off the old self with its practices and have put on the new self, which is being renewed in knowledge after the image of its creator. Here there is not Greek and Jew, circumcised and uncircumcised, barbarian, Scythian, slave, free; but Christ is all, and in all.*

—*Colossians 3:5–11*

REFLECT / We learned yesterday that in heaven's view, when we place our faith in Jesus, we are considered buried with Him and raised with Him. Gone is the old version of us. We've been made alive together with Him. Now we have a new life, a new identity—a new self. We are no longer citizens of this world but citizens of heaven, and we set our minds according to its ways. And so it makes sense for Paul to follow up all these amazing truths with a set of instructions on what to do with all those old earthly habits that sometimes haunt us in our new life with Jesus. After all, in Paul's logic, we shouldn't just *think* on heavenly things instead of earthly things; we should *act* in heavenly ways instead of earthly ways, too.

Paul knows that old habits die hard, so he doesn't just toss out a "good luck!" to these believers in Colossae as they try to grow in their faith. No, he gives specific directions on what to do with the old habits—put them all away.

What does this mean? It means we should put to death the things that once ruled our hearts and minds—our sinful and self-focused behaviors and thoughts, along with "sexual immorality, impurity, passion, evil desire, and covetousness, which is idolatry," as well as "anger, wrath, malice, slander, and obscene talk," not to mention lying. All of these things are markers of a person living according to earthly values, and walking in them only shows alignment with their old life instead of the new life in Jesus. And so Paul rightly calls us to "put off the old self."

One helpful way of understanding "put off" is to remember that this is language commonly used in biblical conversations about clothing. "Putting off" and "putting on" are things a person does when dressing themselves. So Paul is essentially telling us this: walking in those old ways is like walking around in clothes that don't fit you anymore. You are being transformed into the image of Christ, sculpted into what *He* looks like, remember? It doesn't make sense to wear things that wouldn't be fitting for Jesus to walk around in. So whatever wouldn't be fitting for Christ, take it off!

Friend, in the pages ahead, we get to *put on* some pretty amazing things. But we won't be ready to change clothes if we don't first take off the things we have no business walking around in. To prepare yourself, look back at this list and consider what needs to go: "sexual immorality, impurity, passion, evil desire, and covetousness, which is idolatry . . . anger, wrath, malice, slander, and obscene talk," and lying. Which of these are you still wearing?

Here's the good news: our obedience, faithfulness, and fruitfulness in putting off these things is truly possible. And it is made possible by—and *only* by—God as the Holy Spirit and the Word work in us to sanctify us. That is to say, God will continue to make us more and more like Christ. We are *being* renewed all the days of our lives as new creations in Christ (Col. 3:10). What good news! We don't have to muster up the power on our own; in God we have all the power we need to put off anything that needs to go and to put on anything God tells us to put on.

Want even more good news? The clothing God wants us to put on is for anyone, not just for "super-spiritual" Christians. *Anyone* can change out of the old and into the new—rich or poor, servant or master, Greek or Jew, or American! Even people who are at odds with one another (like the people groups Paul mentions in this passage!) can enjoy the same invitation from God to put off the outdated ways of the flesh and walk in the fresh, vibrant, radiant robes of righteousness He has given us in Jesus. This good news is for *all* who have trusted in Christ. No one is outside the redeeming work of Jesus and the riches of His glory. Paul knows this well. Remember who Paul was before he was Paul? Saul. The cold, seething Pharisee becomes the warmest member of a group he once hated. He becomes a follower of Jesus—and not just a follower but an apostle.

You may be thinking, *But I'm a sinner still living in a fallen world. I can't possibly put off all this stuff in the blink of an eye and walk perfectly from now on.* You're correct. You aren't totally free from the pull of sin in your life. Its presence will still show up sometimes. But it doesn't have the power to *make* you say yes to putting it on! Though the presence of sin isn't completely gone yet, God promises that the one who has been made new by the redeeming work of Christ, with a new identity as a Christ follower, *will* continue to grow in her ability to put off the old to make way for the new, which is obedience, fruitfulness, and faithfulness to Jesus's way of doing things. Paul articulates this well in his letter to the church in Thessalonica: "Now may the God of peace himself sanctify you completely, and may your whole spirit and soul and body be kept blameless at the coming of our Lord Jesus Christ. He who calls you is faithful; he will surely do it" (1 Thess. 5:23–24).

He will surely do it, friend. Christ is all and in all for those who have trusted in Him, and we can press on, continuing to make a practice, a daily habit, of putting off the old self and putting on the new self—walking in ways that are fitting of Him. Next, we'll get to enjoy the joy of a wardrobe change as we look at Paul's instructions for what we are to *put on* daily as Christ followers. Get ready to put on the new self, friend!

RESPOND

1 / For a final time, look at this list of the things God calls you to put off: sexual immorality, impurity, passion, evil desire, covetousness (which is idolatry), anger, wrath, malice, slander, obscene talk, and lying. How would you put this list in your own words?

2 / Which items on the list above are your most difficult pieces of "clothing" to put off? List those here and bring them before the Father in prayer as you ask Him to help you put off the old self today and this week.

3 / Consider the things you just confessed to God. What dangers do you put yourself in if you keep walking in this way? What benefits do you miss out on?

4 / According to this passage, who gets the invitation to put off the old self and put on the new? Only some people or anyone? What does this teach you about the Lord—is He partial or impartial?

5 / What does today's passage teach you about God's character? How can you live in response to this aspect of His character today? Because God is _____, I will _____.

PRAY

Father, I thank You that in Christ I get to receive new life, new identity—a new self. I ask for forgiveness for the sins that do not reflect my newness in Christ. If I'm walking in anything that is not fitting of Christ, help me put it off. You know the deepest struggles of my old self, and I pray You'll give me the strength I need to put these things to death. I lay those ways before You Father, and I thank You that Jesus died for those sins, so that I might live differently. An invitation to be brand-new—thank You for extending such a thing to anyone, even me! You are such a welcoming, impartial God. Help me reflect Your character as I show impartiality to all. And as I put off the old self, help me become more like Your Son. I know Your Word tells me that "he who began a good work in you will bring it to completion at the day of Jesus Christ" (Phil. 1:6), and so I trust You will empower me to do the hard work of killing old, sinful habits. I praise You that You will never stop renewing me into the image of Jesus. It's in His precious name that I pray, amen.

EXPLORE MORE

In verse 10 of today's passage, Paul says that as Christ's follow-ers, we have now put on the new self and are being renewed in knowledge after the image of our Creator. Now read Romans 12:2. According to this verse, how does Paul say a person is transformed?

Now read Romans 8:29. To whom or what is the believer being transformed, or conformed to, according to what Paul says in this verse?

Today we learned that although we are saved by the justifying work of Jesus on the cross, this does not mean we will no lon-ger experience the presence of sin while we live on earth. Read Romans 6. How many times does the word "free" show up in relation to sin? What is Paul's point, in your own words? How does our increasing habit of putting off the old self prove that we are, indeed, free from the power of sin?

NEW CLOTHES TO WALK IN

READ / *Put on then, as God's chosen ones, holy and beloved, compassionate hearts, kindness, humility, meekness, and patience, bearing with one another and, if one has a complaint against another, forgiving each other; as the Lord has forgiven you, so you also must forgive. And above all these put on love, which binds everything together in perfect harmony. And let the peace of Christ rule in your hearts, to which indeed you were called in one body. And be thankful. Let the word of Christ dwell in you richly, teaching and admonishing one another in all wisdom, singing psalms and hymns and spiritual songs, with thankfulness in your hearts to God. And whatever you do, in word or deed, do everything in the name of the Lord Jesus, giving thanks to God the Father through him.*

—Colossians 3:12–17

REFLECT / When the COVID-19 pandemic started back in 2020 and the world shut its doors, my husband and I suddenly had extra time together at home. I'm sure you can relate to this sudden extra time at home together if you live with family or roommates. We knew we had a lot of ways we could choose to spend that time, and so we took the opportunity to give some extra focus to God's Word together, which has always been somewhat of a struggle for us to find time to do together. Believe it or not, Colossians was the book we picked.

Of all the sections I've come to love in the book of Colossians, today's passage was the place in Scripture I came back to over and over during the pandemic. With all the stress that came with that season, I needed the reminder of how a Christian handles herself, even amid things like lockdowns and virtual schooling and ever-changing health protocols. And you know what? This passage is still a sweet place I draw from on days when I need to remember as Christ's follower what I am to clothe myself with, even when I just don't feel like it.

As we saw in our last devotional, when we are united to Christ in faith, our response first looks like putting off the old self. Meaning, we throw off the old clothes that were fitted for the mold of this world, and we stop walking in them. Today we'll look at the next response of the Christian: putting on the new self. Meaning, we put on clothes that are fitted for the mold of Jesus, whom we are being shaped into more and more each day.

Before we talk about the new clothes, I want to remind you: *you are no longer a slave to sin.* The old clothes don't have you by the throat! As Paul says in Romans: "We know that our old self was crucified with him in order that the body of sin might be brought to nothing, so that we would no longer be enslaved to sin" (6:6). This means that you don't *have* to act like your old self and you aren't *forced* to walk in your old ways of living. That was true of you before Jesus—you were a slave to sin. You had no choice. But now, you're free from its stranglehold over you. The temptation to sin is still there, but you *no longer have* to say yes to that temptation. You now have the power of the Holy Spirit to say no, to "*lay aside* every encumbrance and the sin which so easily entangles" you (Heb. 12:1 NASB 1995). Sin used to entangle you, friend, and you had no power to fight back or pull it off of you. *Now* you can lay it aside, or as some translations say with vigor, *throw it off*!

And so, as people freed from the sin they once loved and lived out, Paul calls the Christians in Colossae to clothe themselves daily with the righteousness of God, putting on the newness in Christ they have now as His followers. And what does that clothing look like according to today's passage? Compassion, kindness, humility, meekness, patience, forbearance, forgiveness, love, peace, and thankfulness. And how can they grow in these things? Through God's Word, His Spirit, and His people. Notice that Paul says these things come about as we let God's Word dwell in us and also as we teach one another, admonish one another, and sing of God's goodness to one another. Paul knows that the Colossians (and we!) can be very forgetful people, so he tells us that we are to keep on reminding one another of who our God is and what He has done for us through His Son, and that God will keep doing the good work he began in us to sanctify His people, growing us in the ways that evidence people who are filled with the Holy Spirit. People who have put off the old self and have put on the newness in Christ as His followers.

The Colossians weren't the only ones being called to walk in these new clothes. This is a call for us too. This isn't just something we do once after we have trusted in Christ either; daily we are to make a practice of putting off the old self and putting on the new self (1 John 3:4–10). Every day we need Jesus. Every day we need the hope of the gospel to renew us. Every day we need God's Word to remind us of what walking in Christ looks like so that we might obey and walk around in thoughts and actions that are fitting for Him.

When picturing all of this in my own mind, I think of the character Eustace in The Chronicles of Narnia. (I know, we've talked about Narnia a few times in this devotional guide, but who doesn't love that series?) Remember Eustace? He was a beast of a boy on the inside, and so Aslan allows him to become a beast on the outside—a dragon. After a whole lot of time in that dragon skin, not to mention a whole lot of destruction he causes as a flying, angry, fire-breathing monster, Eustace is weary and finally craves to be changed back into a boy. But Eustace can't scratch his own dragon skin off. He needs Aslan to heal him—to take off the dragon skin and transform it back into his original skin.

And you know what? Aslan does just that. He tells Eustace: "You have to let me undress you." With his own claws, Aslan tears off the dragon skin and then immerses Eustace in water. On the other side of the ordeal, Eustace emerges as a boy again, playing and splashing in the water. He says of his restored body: "I was as smooth and soft as a peeled switch and smaller than I had been." When it was time to come out of the water, Eustace finished up the story: "After a bit, the Lion took me out and dressed me . . . in new clothes—the same I've got on now, as a matter of fact."[3]

This is similar to our relationship to sin. Though humans were originally made to be a certain wonderful way, our nature became compromised by sin (Gen. 3), which turned us beastly inside. Sin entangled us to the point of fully dressing us, totally covering us, and completely trapping us, inside and out. We had no power to rip it off. But Jesus did what we could not do. He transformed us from an old dragon creature into something new, or rather, back into what we were always supposed to be. When we emerge on the other side of His rescuing work, we find that, like Eustace, we are softer inside than we used to be, and we finally see ourselves accurately—small compared to others, not larger than life. Soft and humble instead of hard and haughty. New creatures! Back to what a human was always supposed to be. Back to how God created us to be, so that we could dwell with Him forever. And like Eustace, we shouldn't only wear the new clothes at the moment of our conversion. Rather, people should find us walking around in the "new clothes" every day after that. At any point, on any day, we should be able to point to them and say, "Oh, these weren't just given to me on the day I went from beast to believer. I've got them on right now, as a matter of fact. And should the old dragon scales (our sin!) try to find their way to me, I'll throw them right off. Who wants to go back to being trapped in those terrible things?"

Pandemic or not, when I don't want to wear the "new clothes" God tells me to put on. When I don't want to be compassionate, kind, humble, meek, or patient—God's Word helps me remember just how bad the dragon scales were. More than that, the Scriptures remind me that in the strength of the Spirit, I have the power to put off the temptation to go back to the old self and instead put on newness in Christ, the soft Christlike clothes (Col. 3:12). Finally, we are to not only stir up others, but we are also to be stirred up by our brothers and sisters in Christ, encouraging one another to dress rightly every day, continuing to grow in Christlike maturity as we remind one another of Christ and His sacrifice, giving thanks to God through Him, and to keep putting on the new self, our Christlike clothes.

When I don't want to bear with others or forgive my husband, my kids, my brothers and sisters from church, at the grocery store, or on the internet, God's Word empowers me to put on forgiveness, to share in their burden, to bear with them—even if they are beasts to deal with—knowing that Christ did these things for me when *I* was once a beast to deal with. As Christ was to me at my worst, so I have the power to be to others at theirs.

Friend, hear and receive the good news that is true of you today, tomorrow, and always: you're free from the scales. The old self is done. Throw off the old clothes and put on the clothes of Christ and walk in them. Walk in Him today.

RESPOND

1 / As we learned, those in Christ are to put on the new self. Which of these things come naturally to you? Which are harder for you to put on daily? Why?

2 / We know that putting on these things will come easier to us over time as we let God's Word dwell in us daily. What hinders you from dwelling on God's Word? What are some practical ways you can prioritize the intake of God's Word on a daily basis?

3 / Another way to grow in our ability to put on Christlike "clothes" is to teach one another, admonish one another, and sing of God's goodness to one another. To whom are you *offering* your teaching, admonishment, and singing? From whom are you *receiving* teaching, admonishment, and spiritual songs?

4 / What in your life needs to change for you to both offer and receive these things consistently?

5 / Why is it so important that we must be made new creatures with new hearts before we try to walk in new clothes?

6 / What is our primary purpose in life—in both the big and the small things? (See verse 17.)

7 / What does today's passage teach you about God's character? How can you live in response to this part of His character today? Because God is _____, I will _____.

PRAY

God, thank You for transforming me into a new creation who is no longer trapped under the entangling power of sin. Thank You for the newness of life in Christ. I pray that Your Holy Spirit will help me put off my old self. After all, as a new creature, I'm no longer a fit for those terrible clothes. Now that I'm being made more into Your image, help me put on the clothes that fit such a figure—compassion, kindness, humility, meekness, patience, forbearance, forgiveness, love, peace, and thankfulness. When someone acts beastly toward me, help me bear with them and forgive them, as You have done for me when I was once a beast to You. When I face temptation, remind me that I have the power to throw off my ways of thinking and walking in this world. Please give me a desire for Your Word and ideas for how to daily prioritize your Word, so that it might dwell in me richly, and give me opportunities to both give and receive teaching, admonishment, and worship that sings to Your glory. In Jesus's name, amen.

EXPLORE MORE

Read Galatians 5:22–23. List each fruit of the Spirit. Do you see any overlap between the fruit of the Spirit in Galatians and the list here in Colossians? Make note of that here. What does this tell you?

Read Revelation 19:7–8. What, exactly, is the clothing the bride of Christ is found wearing? How does this passage in Revelation connect to today's passage?

As we walk in these things, the Bible teaches that we are evidencing the fact that we are indeed clothed in Christ, covered in His righteousness. On the other side of this world's story, what else will happen in relation to our "clothing"? Use 2 Corinthians 5:2–4 and Revelation 7:9 to help you answer.

In Peter's letter to professing Christians in the book of 2 Peter, he clearly articulates our need for effort in godliness and why this diligent pursuit of holiness is so needed. If you have extra time, read (or listen) to this short book and look for the reasons Peter gives in each of the three chapters for why we should diligently pursue holiness as Christ's followers.

DISPLAYING THE
GOSPEL AT HOME

READ / *Wives, submit to your husbands, as is fitting in the Lord. Husbands, love your wives, and do not be harsh with them. Children, obey your parents in everything, for this pleases the Lord. Fathers, do not provoke your children, lest they become discouraged.*

—Colossians 3:18–21

REFLECT / "But what does that mean for *us*?" If you have kids, you're probably familiar with this question (or if not, you're probably familiar with your kids doing things to test this question). Kids go out into the world, and they learn how the rules work for other people's lives. In some cases, the rules "out there" aren't the same as the rules "in here." In other cases, though, sometimes the rules do cross over.

For example, kids can learn big important truths in a place like church, and while their parents would agree with those big important truths being taught, for a kid, it all still feels sort of general until they cross over into the threshold of their household and things finally start to get specific. What does the big lesson of "love" mean when my brother hits me on the head with a toy? What does "honoring and obeying" really mean when I'm playing my favorite game and her voice comes bounding down the hallway, interrupting all my fun, telling me to clean up my mess before bed-time? Big lessons are important, but every kid eventually needs to know how the lesson applies *here*, for *us*, in *this* household.

You and I aren't too far off from being kids. Especially not in the household of God. In fact, in the Father's household, we're all children (1 John 3:1). And sometimes, as His kids, we need help going from general to specific.

We know we should treat any other believer in Christlike ways, thus creating a loving and orderly environment in God's greater, general household of faith. But what about the people who aren't just "any other believer"? What about the people who live not only in our broader spiritual household but our *literal* household—peo-ple like our spouse? Our kids? What about the people with whom we share food, water, rooms, Wi-Fi, and TV shows? How does the gospel get displayed in those relationships?

Paul helps us with this in the next section of Colossians. In the previous section of Colossians, he helped us understand how to gen-erally live out the gospel in the greater church context. But now it's time to get a little closer to home, learning how our Christlikeness should spill over and out to those immediately around us.

First, he starts with the foundational relationship a household orbits around: the wife and the husband. Then he moves on to talk-ing to the children. At this point we should feel such dignity. Isn't it amazing that God has a specific, direct word to share with all three parties? He doesn't say, "Husbands, tell your wives this instruction when you have time." He doesn't say, "Parents, tell your kids this direction through the grapevine." He puts each instruction between God and the party God wants to speak to. No middlemen! It is so encouraging to know that God doesn't consider anyone second-class in His household. God is impartial. He doesn't show favorites. He knows us personally and present in our every day lives, not far off—He is immanent. And because God is immanent and not far off, He speaks directly to each party as a follower of Christ, because He loves us. Let's look closer at what God has to say to each party. He speaks directly to each party as a follower of Christ.

First up, wives. Wives are called to humbly submit to their husbands. And this is for a reason. As Ephesians tell us, the marriage relationship isn't a random one. It was created to paint a picture of Christ's relationship with the church, where Christ the bridegroom is the head and the church is the body and bride (Eph. 5:22–33). Just as the church joyfully submits to Christ, who has laid down His life for her sake, a wife should joyfully submit to the head of her own household, which is her husband. Paul says this is "fitting." Why? Because as the church family has a head (Jesus), so should the nuclear family, which is patterned after the church. Said another way, to live as if there is not a head of a household in the nuclear family is to paint a picture of a headless church.

Now let's address the elephant in every room when this word comes up. Submission isn't a word our culture likes very much. But here are some things to encourage you if you are a wife.

One, Jesus perfectly submitted all the time. In fact, He lived His whole life in submission to the Father. Jesus is not asking you to do something He didn't do. Nor would He have practiced submission at all if it were a bad thing to do!

Two, submission is a *Christian* virtue, not a female one. *Every single member* of the household of faith must submit themselves to some form of authority. Primarily, submission to God. This allows for human power, like money or possessions or talents or any other resource the Christian has, to not remain unchecked. Submission allows for power to not merely be *accumulated* over time but *given away*. It's assumed that Christians are submitting to one another all the time as a general practice in the greater household of faith, so living it out specifically in your nuclear household should not feel foreign.

Three, Paul doesn't use the word *obey* for a wife, as he does for bond servants or children. He uses the word *submit* because the marriage relationship is different from relationships with bosses or kids. Paul is classifying the relationship as something in its own league.[4] And lastly, the fact that Paul is speaking directly to wives, and not through the husband, means that submission is to be given to your husband voluntarily and willingly, not forced or coerced. The passage does not give the husband clearance to force submission. It is up to the wife to choose to do this as an act of obedience between her and the Lord.

Next up, husbands. As we said before, the marriage relationship pictures Christ and the church, the husband playing the role of head (Eph. 5:22). So, what does the role of "head" mean? In Colossians, we see that it looks like loving his wife in a way that is never harsh. Ephesians would say that this sort of love should mirror the way Christ loves His bride (Eph. 5:25–26). When we look at how Christ loved the church, we see a love that is self-denying and self-sacrificing, putting the lives and needs of others above His own. This means that in order to rightly reflect the gospel story in his household, a husband must deny himself and consider his wife's needs as most important. Instead of demanding that she serve him all the time, he will be the first to serve her. As Christ does for His bride, he will nourish her, protect her, and "die daily" for her. Not to do this would be to tell the wrong story about Jesus and His people. For a husband to avoid loving his wife in this way would be to display a gospel story where Christ demanded the church to die for Him and not the other way around. Or for the harsh husband, it would tell the story of a Savior who is impatient, unloving, or annoyed with His beloved people, which just isn't true. For an inattentive or unprayerful husband, this would paint Jesus as a Savior who does not nourish His body, or intercede for His people, which He clearly does—in fact, He *always* lives to make intercession for His people (Heb. 7:25).

For children, displaying the gospel story looks like obeying their parents. Just as followers of Christ are called to cheerfully obey God, their heavenly Father, kids can tell that story to a watching world. In a world where disobedience and disorder are normal and even considered funny, kids have a real opportunity to showcase what order and fun and flourishing really look like in the family of God!

Last, *parents.* (Though the word used here is "fathers," the original language actually encompasses both father and mother.[5]) Just as every other member of the family should act in such a way that tells a greater story, the same is true of parents. They paint a picture to their kids of what our heavenly Father is like—the Father we've been reconciled to through Christ's gospel work. And so, how do parents paint the right picture of the Father? By not provoking their kids. What does this mean? In the original language "provoke" meant to stir up anger or to irritate. In other words, as parents, we shouldn't pick a fight with our kids or pressure and prod them in such a way that incites an angry response. We shouldn't deliberately evoke their frustration and anger by teasing them, being harsh or sarcastic with them, or doing anything else that would purposefully embitter them toward us. Why? Because our heavenly Father does not operate this way with us. He does not cheerfully afflict His children, nor does He seek to discourage them. To act in such a way tells the wrong story to our kids about God's character.

In all these ways, the gospel should clearly transform every part of our lives, including our households. Jesus is Lord over everyone and everything (Col. 1:15–17), especially His own household, the church. Therefore, the structure of our households and the roles God has given men, women, and children within the family structure should aim to look like that truth. In other words, putting Jesus first means living in our households in a way that fittingly reflects His story. What a precious gift God gives each of us to be given the opportunity to reflect the gospel daily within our homes as His image bearers. What a gift to have a God who is living and active and holds the infinite power to transform every single part of our lives, including our relationships within our own homes. What a gift to have a God who is immanent—involved in every part of our lives, leaving no place untouched by His sovereign care over us.

Friend, if you're looking at your family now, feeling discouraged, take heart: nothing is so big or so small that God can't restore. He is a God of order and restoration. It is His very nature to redeem all things. If you see parts of your household that need some renovation, ask Him. He loves to run a flourishing household, and He can do it in yours. Right now the Father offers us redemption from sin through His Son, and we know that one day He will restore everything once and for all when Jesus returns (Rev. 21).

RESPOND

1 / Which specific instruction in today's passage was hardest for you to hear? Why?

2 / Why is it important for specific nuclear families to tell the larger, general story about God and His people? What is lost if Christian families don't do this?

3 / How can you better reflect the gospel in your home this week?

4 / If you have children, how can you point them to Jesus, and how can you guide them in reflecing the gospel this week also?

5 / What does today's passage teach you about God's character? How can you live in response to part of God's character today? Because God is _____, I will _____.

PRAY

> *God, thank You for making my family a small pattern that points to the larger story of You and Your great work in the world. Help me reflect the gospel this week within my own home. Whether woman, wife, mother, stepmother, sister, aunt, spiritual mother, roommate, granddaughter, or grandmother, You know the role I have in my family, Thank You for caring for me so personally in each of these roles. I pray that the Holy Spirit would help me overcome any resistance toward Your commands so that those who enter my home might make better sense of Your wonderful household and the gospel story that made it possible. I ask for forgiveness when I fail to reflect the gospel within my home, and I trust that as I trust Your pattern for my relationships, I will grow to become more like Jesus. In His precious name, amen.*

EXPLORE MORE

Read Genesis 1:26–28 and Genesis 2:18–25. God is a God of order. Before sin entered into the world, God's good world and everything He made in it were in perfect order, functioning exactly as they should, all the time. After reading these two passages from Genesis, what specific roles were man and women given by God in relationship to each other? What role did they fill in relationship to God's creation?

Read Ephesians 5:22–6:9. Make note of the similarities to our passage we read today that you read in Ephesians. In our marriage and family, what is your primary purpose?

DISPLAYING THE
GOSPEL AT WORK

READ / *Bondservants, obey in everything those who are your earthly masters, not by way of eye-service, as people-pleasers, but with sincerity of heart, fearing the Lord. Whatever you do, work heartily, as for the Lord and not for men, knowing that from the Lord you will receive the inheritance as your reward. You are serving the Lord Christ. For the wrongdoer will be paid back for the wrong he has done, and there is no partiality.*

Masters, treat your bondservants justly and fairly, knowing that you also have a Master in heaven.

—Colossians 3:22–4:1

REFLECT / What does work look like for you? For me, as a way to invest in our community and make a little extra cash, I work for a nonprofit soccer association here in rural Minnesota. It is a joy, and it's also a lot of work. As the only paid person, I take on a lot of the responsibilities the club and its board members would like me to do for them. One of those responsibilities includes helping to manage our big fall fundraiser that brings in most of the income our club needs to function well for the upcoming year. With that fundraiser came the desire, and event anxiety, of it going *well*. I wanted to serve the club itself, and our community that came out to support the club, *well*. I wanted to perform well. I wanted the monetary number at the end of the fundraising to turn out . . . *well*. The motivation in my heart for why I wanted it to go well? Honestly, it was a battle between worldly pride and godly humility. On the pride side of things, I wanted to make myself and the club look good based on the amount of money we raised. On the humility side, I wanted Jesus to look good in me as I worked the event and served those who attended, no matter the amount of funds we raised that evening. I'm happy to report that by God's grace the latter won out, and Jesus gave me such joy and peace that evening to work and serve for His glory and not my own.

I wonder if you have similar struggles with work—whatever work looks like for you. I wonder what sort of battles happen in your heart as you take on a new task or handle a new problem. You, like me, probably want things to go well.

As we see in this new section of Colossians, Paul wants things to go well in our work lives, too. Not well in the worldly sense but well in the gospel-centered sense. For Paul, success in our work environments is measured not by how much money we make or how high on the ladder we climb; it is measured by how we display the gospel.

Before we jump into this passage, let's pause to make sure we understand the context. Let's recall one of the main points we discussed before we began our journey through Colossians: we'll remember the original audience of this letter and when this letter was written. These things matter in how we read and view some of the concepts and words that show up in today's passage.

First, given the time period of Colossians, it is helpful to know that "work" and "home" were spheres of life that often overlapped.

Things are different today where we have a strong separation between work life and personal life. But in the era of the Colossians, the household wasn't just a dwelling place strictly for the family unit. It was a workplace too—where *lots* of workers played their part in the greater household, including servants. This is why we see instructions about work relationships (servant, master) right next to the previous instructions about family relationships (wife, husband, kids, parents). All these parties were part of the same household where "work stuff" and "home stuff" happened at the same time.

While we're talking about context, it is helpful to know that the terms "bondservant/servant" and "master" were often used in the Old Testament to describe many different roles people played in their working relationships. Fast-forward to New Testament times, and we find that in the Roman Empire, bond servants would bind themselves under contract to work in a master's household for about seven years. When the contract was completed, the person was given both freedom and wages the master had saved, and the person was then officially declared free in the eyes of the law and the greater community, able to enter in whatever new job he found the next chapter of his work life.[6] When Paul shares a word for how the gospel should be portrayed in a Christian household, he considers even the servants as members of it and speaks directly to them as fellow believers.

Although our modern household structure and ways of serving in our jobs looks different from the way it looked in New Testament times, Paul's instructions here in Colossians still apply to our general working relationships. The gospel should impact the way we treat one another, whether we are the worker or the boss.

As we saw previously, Paul has already laid out what reflecting the gospel daily looks like as a member of a family. Today we see what reflecting the gospel looks like to a member of the workforce.

First up, employees. Paul says that employees are to obey their earthly authority figure in the workplace, and that's fitting. Earthly authority figures tell the story of a God who is in authority, and so respecting earthly authority, even in the smallest ways, displays respect for God. After all, "there is no authority except from God, and those that exist have been instituted by God" (Rom. 13:1). Notice that Paul doesn't say to simply obey an authority figure; he says to obey with a certain kind of heart: "not by way of eye-service, as people-pleasers, but with sincerity of heart, fearing the Lord" (Col. 3:22).

This means that we must carry out our work with a sincere heart, not seeking to accomplish our work to receive the glory of others, but rather for the glory of God. We shouldn't be only obeying for "eye-service," meaning, only doing the job right when the boss can see us and congratulate us. Rather, we should obey in the shadows, too, because we actually respect the institution of work (and the authority figures that come with it) to begin with and because our heart is actually in it. We should not be seeking to please people but rather aiming to please God in our work. We need the reminder: "You are serving *the Lord Christ*," not merely the person in charge. Our work tells a story about what it's like to be a servant in *His* household, and shouldn't that include joy and diligence? In all these ways and more, working well is about God, not man. In fact, everything we do in this life should ultimately be for God's glory (1 Cor. 10:31).

In fact, Paul goes on to say that in everything, whatever we do, we are to do it for the glory of God. We are to work heartily for Him in the work, roles, and responsibilities He's given us, knowing that our reward in achieving these tasks for His glory will result in the greatest prize a person could ever attain: eternal, resurrected life in heaven with Him. Or, in Paul's words, "inheritance." What is Paul getting at? He is making clear that God sees and rewards hard work done unto Him, even if earthly authority figures don't recognize or reward it. Here's how Paul would word it in Ephesians: "Whatever good anyone does, this he will receive back from the Lord, whether he is a bondservant or is free" (Eph. 6:8). And the reverse is also true with any wrong we do in our jobs: "The wrong-doer will be paid back for the wrong he has done, and there is no partiality" (Col. 3:25).

As an employer, the same is true. Just as God sees the work of an employee and reciprocates fairly based on her work, God sees and rewards employers for how they treat those under their authority. Who is under your authority today? Perhaps you have a job where you manage other people. Or maybe your hard work is in the realm of mothering, where a host of little ones look to you each day for guidance and teaching. Whoever it is, you are called to reflect the gospel by treating them justly and fairly, showing no partiality (favoritism), just as our Father in heaven deals with us and shows no partiality (Gal. 3:28; Rom. 2:11; Col. 3:11).

Two attributes (characteristics) of our God that we see over and over in His Word are that He is a just judge and He is impartial. When it comes to the workplace, His character remains the same in these ways. And as we reflect His character in the workplace, we get to be a living picture of what kind of Master He is. What an honor that is! As God's servant, our aim as we interact with those who work under our authority is to model this well. We want to reveal just how wonderful Christ is, the Master and head of His church, and the ways He interacts and deals with His servants.

In some ways we are all workers who stand under someone else's authority. In other ways, we are the boss, and others are under our authority. Either way, we are called to tell the story of what work is like in the household of God. How is that storytelling going for you in your work life? If you find yourself discouraged as you evaluate the ways you handle being a worker or a boss and the story that tells the world about God, our Master, and we, His servants, remember this, friend: there is no part of our lives that God can't redeem through the gospel! He is immanent in the lives of His people. Meaning, God is near! He is involved in every single part of the lives of His people. This is good news, friend! God uses all things for His glory, even your mistakes or missteps in work.

As God grows you to better reflect Him in this area of your life, remember the privilege it is to be His hands and feet in our workplaces. I pray that as you enter the work He has entrusted to you, your aim would be to keep putting Jesus first: doing your work with excellence, for His glory, and with a sincere heart that serves the needs of others above your own—for this is how our Master served us!

RESPOND

1 / Do you identify more as a worker or a boss? Or both? Why?

2 / In what ways do you sometimes work for "eye-service" or as "people-pleasers"? Why is this an unsustainable way to approach work over the long haul?

3 / In your own words, explain how being a good worker tells the right story about being a servant in God's household. How does being a good authority figure tell the right story about Christ, our Master?

4 / What does today's passage teach you about God's character? How can you live in response to part of God's character today? Because God is _____, I will _____.

5 / Whether a worker or a boss, how can you better reflect the gospel in your work this week?

PRAY

Immanent, heavenly Father, who is near and involved in every part of our lives, thank You for giving me yet another environment to tell the story of how wonderful You are. It is a joy to be a worker in Your loving household. Help me reflect this truth in my workplace. Help me work heartily for You, God, not seeking the approval of man but aiming to please You in the work that You have put in front of me. As a worker, help me put Jesus first as I serve my employer for Your glory. As a boss, help me put Jesus first as I serve those under my authority justly and fairly, knowing that this reflects You, the Master who treats us justly and fairly, too. Forgive me for the ways I've failed to reflect the gospel in my work life. Give me humility to apologize to those in my workplace when I do not treat them in a way that pleases You, gives You glory, or tells the right story about Your household. Restore my workplace, Father. Redeem the places You've called me to reflect the hope of the gospel for Your glory. In Jesus's name, amen.

EXPLORE MORE

Read the parable of the servant master in Luke 12:35–38.

• *When you think about the assumed roles of servant and master, why is this parable that Jesus shares with the disciples so surprising?*

• *What is Jesus trying to teach them through this story of the servant master?*

• *Find another place or two in Scripture where Jesus describes Himself as a servant King.*

In Matthew 20:1–6, read the parable of the workers in the vineyard. Here we see that the master shows the attributes of being just and fair. But there is also another attribute on display in this parable in addition to his justice and fairness.

• *What is the extra attribute on display in this parable (v. 15)?*

• *Why do some of the workers experience frustration over this attribute?*

• *How does this parable challenge you, or encourage you?*

CONTINUE STEADFASTLY

READ / *Continue steadfastly in prayer, being watchful in it with thanksgiving. At the same time, pray also for us, that God may open to us a door for the word, to declare the mystery of Christ, on account of which I am in prison—that I may make it clear, which is how I ought to speak.*

Walk in wisdom toward outsiders, making the best use of the time. Let your speech always be gracious, seasoned with salt, so that you may know how you ought to answer each person.

—*Colossians 4:2–6*

REFLECT / I love gardening. Although I love it, it is a lot of work. If you're a gardener, you know this well. I get lots of help throughout the summer from my parents who are longtime gardeners and from my husband, and of course our little ones "help" too. Though it is labor-intensive, the work we put in during spring and summer is always worth it we get to reap the things we sowed months earlier. Seeing God, the Sustainer of all things, grow a bountiful harvest for us to enjoy year after year reminds me that all of the time and toil are worth the effort in the end.

Some of the things we like to grow include tomatoes, bell peppers, onions, jalapeno peppers, and herbs. And one of my favorite things to make with these crops is pico de gallo. Fresh pico de gallo straight from your garden is so satisfying to enjoy. But one thing that must always be added to finish or complete the pico is salt. Salt adds the final touch, and it definitely enhances the flavor. Add too little salt, and the flavor just isn't there yet. Add too much, and you basically ruin the entire batch. It's an essential ingredient but must be portioned with care.

As Paul begins to wrap up his letter to the Colossians, he tells them to continue in steadfastness. He asks them to steadfastly pray not only for *their* own maturity and faithfulness to Jesus but also for *his* faithfulness to share the gospel as he walks through any open doors God might have him enter. He asks them to pray for his speech to be clear as he proclaims the good news about Jesus when God gives him the opportunity. He asks them to pray for not just themselves but for him, a leader.

First, reading this makes me wonder: *Do I pray for my own maturity and faithfulness in a steadfast way? Do I pray that God would grant me the words I need to share the gospel with lost friends?* And second, it makes me wonder: *Do I pray fervently for the faithfulness and boldness of Christian leaders in my life, too, that they'd also be faithful as they boldly share the gospel?* If you're anything like me, you probably forget that your leaders need these prayers, too—probably because we forget that our leaders are human, like us, having their own challenges, sin tendencies, struggles, and temptations! We forget that we all have a battle against spiritual warfare (Eph. 6:12). We forget that we all have an enemy who seeks to kill and destroy God's people (1 Pet. 5:8). For all of these reasons and more, even the most seemingly "strong" or mature Christians need our prayers. After all, if the *apostle Paul* asked for prayer in these ways, how much more do the leaders in your life need prayer?

Finally, we see Paul command the Colossians to walk in wisdom. Why do they need wisdom exactly? Paul lays it out for us: for their interactions with outsiders, for the way they handle their tongue, and for the way they handle their time.

First, Paul wants them to be discerning and wise when it comes to outsiders—meaning non-Christians. He also wants them to be aware and wise in the way they handle the false teaching they are experiencing not only outside of the church right now but inside the church as well.

Next, Paul understands that our time on this earth is finite, so he prays that these believers will be wise in the way they handle their minutes and days in this world. How convicting is that when you think about how much time most of us spend on things like our devices and social media? It's certainly convicting for me! It makes us pause and evaluate what we are allowing to consume our time, and on the flip side, how much of *other* people's time we are demanding that they spend on us when we share things online. These Colossians didn't have any of that back then to consume their time. If they were in need of a reminder not to waste time, just think of how much more we need the reminder. Paul's desire for them is the same for us: that we'd be given the wisdom we need to make the best use of our time, walking in obedience to God.

Finally, Paul wants them to be ready to respond to others wisely when it comes to their tongue—with graciousness and speech that are seasoned with salt. Seasoned well so that they will know how to answer someone.

When it comes to wisdom with outsiders, how is our Christian culture doing these days? How do we treat the lost outside of our midst and any bad teaching within our midst? In many ways, I've seen Christians fighting with lost people online about everything under the sun! You too? It seems Christians are on high alert for disagreement with lost folks *outside* of their faith community but *not* on alert about the kinds of misleading teaching or theology that exists inside their own faith community. This is not wisdom, for it sets the target on the wrong back. Wisdom with outsiders means inviting them in to hear the gospel, and wisdom with insiders means defending the truth at all cost. And yet in our day and age, it is so tempting to defend ourselves against the lost communities while keeping the invitation open to flagrant sin within the body of Christ. Or, as Paul would say in another letter: "For what have I to do with judging outsiders? Is it not those inside the church whom you are to judge?" (1 Cor. 5:12).

This is convicting for us all: In what ways have we been practicing a backwards wisdom? In what ways have we defended ourselves against the lost culture around us, blaming it for all our problems and judging those on the other side of the church's wall, while allowing sin within our faith community to go unchecked, failing to place blame where it is actually due? Wisdom requires both.

When it comes to practicing wisdom with our time and our tongue, we could ask similar questions. In what ways have we been using these things unwisely? And knowing that we'll be held accountable for every careless hour or word we use in this life (Matt. 12:36), how can we grow in wisdom?

As we briefly saw before, Paul gives us a clue with something as simple as salt. To help our responses toward outsiders and insiders, our speech should be seasoned with salt. Salt is both a preserver and a provider of flavor. We are to be the salt of the earth as Jesus teaches His disciples during His Sermon on the Mount (Matt. 5:13). When it comes to life, in a world where sin is the agent of decay, we should be agents that preserve. In a world that is sour or bland, we should be flavorful. When the words flying around us tear down, we should preserve the one who is being torn down and build them up. When the speech circulating in our neighborhood or on social media is full of disgusting talk, the flavor coming out of our mouth should be sweet. Yet many of us have lost our saltiness, and we use our words and time just like the rest of the world. Just as when salt loses its taste, if our speech and lives are not seasoned well with graciousness and thankfulness to God, they are worthless (Matt. 5:13). We cannot be the salt of the earth if our speech is not pleasing to God. But if we remain salty, we will remain wise!

Paul prays for steadfastness in all these things because it's *hard* to remain bold in sharing the gospel, wise in our treatment with outsiders and insiders, and salty in our speech and our time. And yet, as followers of Jesus, this kind of faithfulness is possible. Like Paul, we can endure in prayer for one another as we seek to do these things in the power of the Holy Spirit. It really is possible to be steadfast in carrying out the Great Commission, steadfast in walking wisely with the time we have on earth, and steadfast in reflecting Jesus in all things, including our speech! And as we do this consistently, you know what it proves? That Jesus is highest and best in our life.

To do this, friend, we need one another. We need other believers nearby to remind us to keep going. We need someone spurring us on as we seek to walk wisely in this world. Who is that person for you? And who might need you to be this kind of person for them? Go find them, because if Paul needed these prayers, so do we!

RESPOND

1 / How do we grow in wisdom as Christians? Read Proverbs 1:7; 1 Corinthians 1:18–25; and James 1:5 to help explain your answer.

2 / Of these things, which is the hardest for you to remain steadfast in: sharing the gospel, wisdom with outsiders, wisdom with insiders, time management, speech, living as salt and light? Why?

3 / What new insights did you learn about salt, or about steadfast Christian living, in this passage? How does this help you walk more wisely?

4 / What does today's passage teach you about God's character? How can you live in response to part of His character today? Because God is
_____, I will _____.

PRAY

Father, thank You for being the ultimate source of wisdom and steadfastness. Thank You for not keeping these things to Yourself but giving wisdom generously to those who ask. I ask You to give me discernment and wisdom right now. Help me learn how to walk wisely according to Your will. It is hard for me to remain steadfast. But I pray by the power of Your Spirit that You'll help me remain faithful in the ways I share the gospel, the way I spend my time, and the way I use my tongue. No matter whom I come in contact with, let my words be seasoned with salt so that I might be an agent of preservation and flavor in a world that is decaying and sour. Help me see when I'm starting to walk the foolish way of the world instead of the ways of Your Son, who is the true wisdom of God. Help me become more like Him, growing wiser by the day! In His name, amen.

EXPLORE MORE

In Exodus 25–31, God gives specific instructions to Moses to relay on to God's chosen people, the Israelites. These six chapters are full of complete, detailed instructions for how they are to set up the place where the priests would be able to meet with God. This includes detailed instructions for all the many objects that were to be used in worship, as well as many detailed instructions for the priests themselves, even down to their garments. This leads to today's Explore More passage. Read the complete, detailed instructions God gave Moses regarding the anointing oil and incense for the tent of meeting so that God could dwell with His people in Exodus 30:34–38, paying special attention to verse 35. What further insight does this passage give you about the meaning of "seasoned with salt"?

To learn more about how to wisely engage outsiders, consider 1 Timothy 3:7; 1 Thessalonians 4:11–13; and 1 Peter 2:12–17; 3:14–17. What do these passages teach you about how the church should conduct itself among outsiders?

THE GOODNESS OF THE FAMILY OF GOD

READ / *Tychicus will tell you all about my activities. He is a beloved brother and faithful minister and fellow servant in the Lord. I have sent him to you for this very purpose, that you may know how we are and that he may encourage your hearts, and with him Onesimus, our faithful and beloved brother, who is one of you. They will tell you of everything that has taken place here.*

Aristarchus my fellow prisoner greets you, and Mark the cousin of Barnabas (concerning whom you have received instructions—if he comes to you, welcome him), and Jesus who is called Justus. These are the only men of the circumcision among my fellow workers for the kingdom of God, and they have been a comfort to me.

—Colossians 4:7–11

REFLECT / When I became a mom, I quickly realized how little I appreciated my mom and dad growing up. Raising tiny humans is no cakewalk, and I would say I was a particularly tough kid. I was super independent, didn't take no for an answer, and knew how to push my parents (and little brother's) buttons. I was a little lost sinner who needed saving. Looking back, I am so thankful for all the ways my parents continued to love and support me, even with how difficult I was. More than that, I am so thankful that God saved that little sinner!

So, since becoming a mom myself, I appreciate my parents even more as they continue to love and support me and my own children now. Becoming a parent is challenging in so many ways, and since having our second and, most recently, our third sweet child, I have become more and more aware of my lack of sufficiency.

Transitioning from two to three children has been easy in some ways and hard in others. For example, the newborn nuances are easier to handle and gauge, because it's our third baby. You know the deal when it comes to feeding and changing. But juggling the baby's needs on top of the needs of the older two, especially the three-year-old, who really reminds me of little sinner Courtney at times, has brought me to my knees in tearful prayers more than ever—which has forced me to rely on God a whole lot more (which is a very good position to be in!) and on others more often, too. By nature I'm a doer. I'd rather just do it myself than feel like I'm burdening someone else with my stuff. I'd rather handle the problem than ask for help. So this season of life has been extremely frustrating at times but also humbling. As much as I like to think I am at times, I'm not in control over everything, and I'm definitely not self-sufficient. I can no longer depend on just myself to get through the day.

Though this phase is hard, if I'm being honest, it's teaching me to be exactly where I should be: humble and lowly, crying out at the feet of Jesus for help. Trusting in His sufficiency when I run out of steam. Leaning on Him for my every need. This is the posture of a Christian!

That's where the sweetness of this passage comes in. We cannot do it all—even the apostle Paul couldn't. The only one who is self-sufficient is God. He needs nothing from us. Nothing. He sustains Himself, still gets all the glory even without us, and He sustains everything else (Col. 1:17). We were made to depend on the Sustainer of all things. Let me repeat that: we were made to depend on Him. He is not frustrated or burdened that we need to depend on Him. He delights in our depending on Him. He *made* us that way because He loves to be our help when we need it. As we go about our days, we need His Holy Spirit. We need His Word. And we need His people!

As brothers and sisters in Christ, we need one another. To worship God together, to disciple one another, to speak the truth in love to one another, to pray for one another as we talked about in yesterday's devotional, to comfort one another, to encourage one another, to partner with one another in ministry, to sharpen one another and hold one another accountable—all so that we might enjoy life in Christ and be kept from falling away from the faith into sin. And even if we do fall, we need godly relationships to help us get back on track and to spur one another on in Christ.

We see almost every single one of these examples of brothers and sisters in Christ doing life together in today's passage. Paul describes five men: Tychicus, Onesimus, Aristarchus, Mark, and Justus who are helping him in his ministry to advance the gospel of Jesus, and here we see the goodness of the family of God. Isn't it amazing to know that even Paul needed these siblings in God's household to help him along? God shows His kindness and His amazing grace to us in so many ways, and one of those ways is through giving us such siblings.

If you had a list like Paul's, who would be on the list? I imagine the names wouldn't be Tychicus, Onesimus, Aristarchus, Mark, or Justus—but those blanks would be filled in with other names. For Paul, these were the guys who served alongside him as he labored for the church. They were brothers in their level of closeness, battling through the hard times together and laughing through the good times. They were Paul's comrades, his fellow ministers and instructors in the faith. One of them even sat in prison with him. So I'll ask you again: Who would be on your list? Who has helped you along in hard seasons? Who has ministered alongside you in your church? Who has tended to your needs in the hard seasons and celebrated with you in the joyful moments? Who has sat in the trench with you when you needed it and also instructed you in the faith when you needed it?

If you don't have a list like this, let's start making it, friend. I need to add some to my list too! Because we were meant to do life together. To be in community together. To be a part of a unified local church family carrying out the Great Commission together despite our diverse backgrounds and cultures. We were meant to take on both the storm and the breeze together, serving our King Jesus as fellow workers for the kingdom of God.

Let us humbly learn from the words of Paul here and depend on God and on the community of believers God has given us. Let us walk obediently with God, carrying out His Great Commission to advance the gospel and grow the kingdom of God together in our churches, schools, workplaces, park playgrounds, grocery stores, communities, neighborhoods, towns, cities, states, nations, and continents. God has His work for us to do right where He has us.

And we can't do it without a list like this one here in Colossians. We need our brothers and sisters in arms to do the job well. Go forth and make your list, friend. You need the people God wants you to write into those blanks. Start your list, add to your list, or drop yourself into someone else's list—there is life to be lived for His glory alongside His beloved people.

RESPOND

1 / As you make your list of names, what emotions flood you? Shame that the list isn't long enough? Frustration that you haven't found the right church home yet, so that you might meet the people who could fill your list? Conviction that you haven't filled the blanks on someone else's list? No matter how you feel, remember: God loves to help you. He made you so that you might be dependent on Him in everything, even in building these friendships. He is not frustrated or burdened that you need Him for this! Do not run or hide from God; just ask Him to help. Invite Him in, however you're feeling, and petition Him to help you develop the relationships He wants you to have.

2 / Think of someone in your church family who might need some help right now. Write their name down here and pray for them. Then reach out to them. Ask them how they are doing and what you could do to help them in the season God has them in right now. Encourage them and comfort them with God's truth.

3 / As Paul writes this letter, he is carrying out his call to share the gospel. Where does God have you right now that you could use as an opportunity to share the good news of Jesus with those around you?

4 / What does today's passage teach you about God's character? How can you live in response to this aspect of His character today? Because God is _____, I will _____.

PRAY

Father, thank You for Your church! Thank You for making me, and every other Christian, the kind of creature who needs others in order to faithfully live out Your call on our lives. I pray You'll give me the relationships I need to live out the Christian life. I also pray You'll give me and all Your people the boldness we need to share the good news of the gospel and advance Your kingdom. I am amazed that You do this through the local church. You know my specific struggles with the church, and I lay those before You right now, trusting You to help me move forward. Ultimately, I know that it pleases You when I am in community with other believers, carrying out Your Great Commission alongside them. I can't do it alone! I pray right now for anyone in my life who has a list of empty blanks. Would You make me someone who could fill one of their blanks? If they are in a trench, give me eyes to see so that I might sit with them. If they are sharing the gospel and need help, give me the courage I need to join them in their efforts. If they are afraid to come to church, please give them the courage to walk through the doors and give me an eagerness to welcome them into your family. If they are hurting, or if they have even been wronged by the church, I pray for healing and forgiveness. Please draw them to Yourself through Your Word, and give them fresh faith and a new desire to be in community with believers and join Your body, the church, once again.

EXPLORE MORE

Read Hebrews 10:19–25. What does the author of Hebrews have to say about being a part of the family of God? What reasons does the author give that reflect the benefits of doing life with fellow believers?

Read Romans 16 and make note of all the people Paul mentions by name and the role they play in his kingdom work. What similarities do you see between that list and this list in Colossians? What differences do you see? How does this encourage you to develop a network of other believers who will help you walk with God and advance His kingdom?

REMEMBER MY CHAINS

READ / *Epaphras, who is one of you, a servant of Christ Jesus, greets you, always struggling on your behalf in his prayers, that you may stand mature and fully assured in all the will of God. For I bear him witness that he has worked hard for you and for those in Laodicea and in Hierapolis. Luke the beloved physician greets you, as does Demas. Give my greetings to the brothers at Laodicea, and to Nympha and the church in her house. And when this letter has been read among you, have it also read in the church of the Laodiceans; and see that you also read the letter from Laodicea. And say to Archippus, "See that you fulfill the ministry that you have received in the Lord."*

I, Paul, write this greeting with my own hand. Remember my chains. Grace be with you.

—*Colossians 4:12–18*

REFLECT / What do we do when we receive good news? The news of a baby being born, a family member getting engaged, a couple who recently got married? One way we express the significance of this news is to share it! Smartphones and social media today make sharing much faster and easier than in the days of Paul. In those days most news was delivered in the form of a letter by hand, walked to the next city to be shared, and then passed on once more.

As we wrap up our final devotional in our journey through Colossians (Yay! We did it, friend!), we see Paul's urgency in sharing this news he writes to the Colossians. Paul is not only concerned with the health of the local church in Colossae but in the surrounding cities too and the churches that have been planted there as well. He wants the gospel message to continue on, reminding the other churches in the surrounding area to hold fast to the hope they have in Christ, not wavering in their faith that is secure in Him, not adding to the finished work of Christ that many false teachers are trying to establish within the church at the time, and not forgetting who their Savior is: the Creator and Sustainer of all things, Jesus.

As we explore this last section, we see Paul laying out how he wants the gospel to advance, greeting those who have partnered with him in the gospel, and offering a final encouragement to the Colossians as he closes his letter to them.

As he finishes up, Paul ends by telling the Colossians to "remember [his] chains." Though we could spend the remainder of our devotional time talking about a few things in this section, I want to spend the last part of today's devotional focusing on this phrase.

Paul is currently imprisoned on house arrest in Rome. Why? Because He has proclaimed the gospel of Jesus Christ and invited others to exercise faith in Him. But the authorities did not like that, and so they threw him in jail. He is currently suffering and being persecuted for the sake of the gospel. He asks the Colossians to remember this.

In a world where we'll do just about anything *not* to feel uncomfortable, this seems like an uncomfortable request. Who wants to remember the hard stuff? Who wants to picture terrible things happening to people? And yet Paul says remember. *Remember your brother over here, persecuted and in chains. Don't forget about me.*

Our sensibilities are pricked by this—am I right? We want to look the other way. We'd rather just turn on our favorite show—Netflix and chill—and forget about the suffering of our brothers and sisters, who, like Paul, suffer in chains around the world right this minute because of their faithfulness to Christ. And yet the Scripture is the same to us as it was to the Colossians. We must fight our instinct to dismiss the uneasy thought of our spiritual family in prison cells, and we must *remember their chains.*

So, why should we remember those who are being persecuted for the sake of the gospel? There's a lot to unpack in this question, but let me just share a few reasons it is good to remember the suffering and persecution happening to our brothers and sisters in Christ.

First, paying attention to the suffering of our brothers and sisters helps us get outside of our self-absorbed nature. We are so prone to selfishness. We often feel like the problems we face are the end of the world. That's not to say we should think our problems are not real or difficult, because they certainly can be. But shifting our focus off of ourselves and onto others reminds us that although we have our own problems and troubles, some brothers and sisters are struggling and suffering in many ways too—and their example could even school us on how to remain faithful under hardship. Their situation also reminds us that we aren't alone in our troubles, even though they may look different. Knowing the suffering of our brothers and sisters helps us battle against our own selfishness.

Second, knowing how our brothers and sisters are suffering helps us better pray for one another. Paul shows us how to pray for one another in a general sense at the beginning of Colossians (Col. 1:3, 9), but knowing about the chains of persecution at the end of the book gives us one super-specific way we can pray. And why should we pray? The Bible is full of examples of people interceding for one another, and the greatest example we see is Jesus interceding for us on the cross and also in heaven! The Holy Spirit also intercedes on our behalf to God; being an interceder and helping us in our weakness is one of the most vital roles the Holy Spirit plays in the life of the Christian (Rom. 8:26). So in our interceding for others in prayer, we reflect both God the Son and God the Holy Spirit! On top of that, we see that praying for the persecuted is something the church does instinctively. In the case of Peter, the prayers of believers were answered by God, and Peter was busted out of jail by an angel (Acts 12)! But even if believers are not delivered in an earthly sense from their chains, they will be in a heavenly sense, and God still finds our intercession deeply pleasing (Ps. 141:2; Rev. 5:8; 8:3–4).

Third, knowing the persecution of our brothers and sisters helps us to remember the Savior—particularly that of all the levels of suffering, He has suffered the greatest amount for our sake. When He was separated from God as He died on the cross for our sin, when He was spat on and shamed publicly, He was persecuted in the greatest possible way. And yet He still accomplished the work God called Him to do. Remembering the chains our brothers and sisters in Christ wear for the sake of the gospel helps us remember the gospel story at large. It helps us recall Jesus, who through wearing chains Himself, broke the chains of sin that once enslaved us. He wore them, He bore them, He tore them, and then He triumphed over them victoriously. Such is the fate of any who suffer for His name!

Fourth, remembering the persecution of our brothers and sisters around the world helps give us a global mindset instead of just a local or national mindset. Persecuted Christians are in all sorts of countries, all over the world. Though this is a hard truth to think about, it's also evidence that the gospel's message is going forth into all nations. Faithful witnesses are encompassing the globe, and remembering their situation helps us recall that Jesus is the King of all nations, not just our nation. It's easy to get wrapped up in pride over the particular country we are a part of, isn't it? And seeking the good of our country is no sin, of course. But in the end, nations rise and fall, and our real country of citizenship, our true home, is the new heaven and earth where we will dwell with God forever, where He will be our God and we will be His people for all of eternity (Rev. 21:3). We ultimately belong to the kingdom of God, whose citizens can be from any country, so long as they confess Christ. King Jesus reigns without borders, His faithful followers coming from every type of people group. God has always had a plan to bring the gospel to all nations. So, on the days we find ourselves interested in only *our* family, *our* neighborhood, *our* state, or *our* country, remembering the chains of persecuted Christians in other countries helps expand our gaze to God's gaze, which covers the whole earth.

And finally, remembering the chains of other believers gives us a picture of what it means to put Jesus first in our lives. Most of us struggle to put Jesus first simply due to distraction or busyness. But our brothers and sisters facing persecution offer us a much more important question: Will we put Jesus first when the threat isn't merely busyness but social shame, legal ramifications, or even physical pain? As we meditate on Jesus, who is highest and best, my prayer is that our answer will be yes, no matter the cost.

As our journey through the book of Colossians concludes, set aside some time today to pray for the persecuted church around the world. I challenge you to join me in adding the persecuted church and those partnering in ministry with the persecuted and underground churches in the world into part of your daily prayer life. Join me also by praying for someone in your local church who is also suffering right now, and reach out to them, letting them know you are praying for them. There is rich fruit when we pray for one another, encourage one another, and point one another to Christ as we share in our sufferings and bear one another's burdens.

RESPOND

1 / Have you ever consistently prayed for the persecuted church? Why or why not? Why is this sort of intercession a particularly difficult practice for Christians who live in free countries?

2 / We'd expect Paul to downplay his prison situation, or not mention it, because it's uncomfortable. Yet he brings it up and pulls it into the light, asking people to pray for him and remember him. What particular issue in your life has you imprisoned, or in "chains"? How can you follow Paul's example—instead of hiding or downplaying, how might you pull this thing into the light, asking for help and prayer? The Colossians were the people Paul appealed to for help and prayer. Who is that for you?

3 / In what new ways have you learned that Jesus is highest and best in this devotional? How might you go about putting Him first in your daily life more consistently?

4 / What does today's passage teach you about God's character? What part of God's character has been most impactful to learn about as you've studied Colossians as a whole?

5 / How can you live in response to these aspects of God's character today? Because God is _____, I will _____.

PRAY

God, I thank You for the faithful brothers and sisters around the world who have been obedient to share the good news of the gospel, often at great risk to themselves and their families. I pray for the persecuted church right now. I ask for Your mercy and protection over them—that You will sustain their strength and release them from their bondage. You know each and every person who is suffering for the sake of the gospel in ways I never will. Please guard them from the schemes of the enemy and embolden them. Encourage their hearts in the eternal hope that they have in Jesus. I also pray for the brothers and sisters in my local church who are facing suffering of various kinds. I pray that You will draw near to them—that Your presence will be a comfort and that You will sustain them through this season of hardship. I pray that in their suffering, they will glorify You. Ultimately, I pray that they will continue to put You first, no matter the cost. And that I will, too. Jesus, You are worth it. In Your precious name, Jesus, amen.

CONCLUSION

Friend! We did it! Over the last twenty-one days we have spent time soaking in the rich truths offered to us from God in the book of Colossians and meditating on the surpassing worth of Christ. *A whole book of the Bible.* We did it together.

I pray that this devotional study has encouraged you and challenged your heart. I pray it has reminded you of just how wonderful, unique, valuable, and amazingly set apart Christ is compared to everything else, allowing you to see Him on full display—preeminent. He is our greatest joy. He is above all things. He is the image of God. He created all things. He sustains all things. He sustains you. He is eternal. He is faithful. He is sufficient. He is worthy to live for and even worthy to die for, should persecution come our way. I pray that seeing all this about Jesus has helped you put Him first in your life, because He's worthy of that top spot in all of our lives!

I also pray that this study has reminded you that false teaching is real, and it can destroy a person's faith. Paul cared so much about throwing out anything that might be added to Jesus for our salvation—and in our day and age, we are just as susceptible to teaching that tells us to add to the gospel! I pray that you and I will take heed of this and be alert for anything that would come up against the grace poured out on the cross. Let us hold fast to the confession of our faith in Jesus, not swaying or being carried away by every false doctrine that comes along in this world.

Jesus alone is worthy of all of our worship, and nothing could ever be added to His justifying work on the cross to save sinners or His glorious resurrection that seals the promise of eternal life for those who love and trust Him. Nothing! I pray that this book has reminded you that we as believers have no greater hope than the power of the resurrection, knowing that just as Jesus was raised to life, defeating sin and death once for all, we too will be raised to life with Him one day. Christ is our hope in this life and in death.

I also pray you've discovered that who Jesus is has implications for every part of our lives. Just as Paul addresses how Jesus should transform every part of their lives to the Colossians, we should evaluate how Jesus is transforming the posture we take within our homes, in our communities, in our workplaces, in our church, and in our own hearts.

As we completed this devotional study together, I pray that you were challenged to show up to God's Word daily. My hope is that you searched the Scriptures first for your answers in the reflection questions (and Explore More sections) each day, and that you have a greater desire to spend time communing with God in His Word and in prayer. I pray that this little book has helped you grow in the knowledge of who our great God is, and because of this knowledge, you've grown in your love for Him.

And finally, I pray that your daily Bible reading won't end here, friend. Rather, I hope that through this guide, you feel better equipped and encouraged to fight for and desire these precious and holy moments communicating with God in His Word and in prayer daily, no matter how busy your day might be. Trust me, I am right there with you fighting for these moments, too.

So friend, as our journey together through Colossians comes to a close, take a few moments to answer these final reflection questions and pray, thanking God for His Word and your time spent studying His Word through this powerful book of the Bible. It was such a joy and an honor to do this alongside you, friend. Jesus is highest and best. He is our greatest joy. He is our greatest hope. He is surpassingly worthy above all things. Our servant King and humble Savior. Keep pursuing to know Him and love Him more, friend. There is no greater joy and pursuit than that. Grace and peace.

RESPOND

1 / How has the book of Colossians taught you or reminded you about the nature and character of God? Make a list of what God is like as you've seen His character and nature highlighted throughout the book of Colossians. Praise Him for who He is.

2 / Think back to the introduction of this devotional study. On page 6, you were asked about what you were most looking forward to about this Bible study, and you were also asked to set one attainable goal for yourself as we journeyed through Colossians together. What was that goal, and did you meet it? Did you enjoy what you were most looking forward to? Did God grow you in any other ways as you completed this devotional study?

3 / Also on page 6, you were asked about your greatest hope for this journey, along with your greatest fear, if any. How would you answer these two questions now that you've completed the study? How did God work these hopes and fears out as we journeyed through Colossians together?

4 / Summarize the book of Colossians in a few sentences. What is the point of this letter from Paul to the Colossians? Why is this letter to the Colossians relevant to us today?

5 / Of all the attributes of God that you've explored in this journey, which one(s) stands out to you the most? How will you move forward in light of this? Because God is _____, I will

_____.

PRAY

God, I thank You for Your Word! Your Word gives life to the believer. It is a lamp to my feet. Your Word is right, true, and good. And so I thank You for the opportunity to learn more about who You are through a whole book of the Bible found in Your Word. Thank You for revealing Yourself through it! And thank You for giving me Jesus, who is highest and best. Thank You for sending Him to save me—to save us all. Thank You for all He is for me and all He's done for me in His life, death, burial, and resurrection. There is no greater love than this.

Jesus, You are matchless. I thank You for being the firstborn over all creation, that everything was created by You, through You, and for You. I thank You that You are before all things, and by You all things hold together. Thank You, Jesus, that You are the head of the church. You are the alpha and omega—the beginning and the end and the firstborn from the dead. I pray that Your Holy Spirit will continually help me place You as the central and highest part of my life. You deserve first place today, tomorrow, and all the days of my life. It's in your precious name, Jesus, that I pray, amen.

What's next? Spend some time today or the next few days thinking about what book of the Bible you want to read or study next. There really is no wrong answer to this, friend! "All Scripture is breathed out by God and profitable for teaching, for reproof, for correction, and for training in righteousness, that the man [and woman] of God may be complete, equipped for every good work" (2 Tim. 3:16–17). So no matter what book of the Bible you choose to read or study next, all of it is useful and good and can and will be used for His glory and your good. His Word cannot and will not return void in your life!

Is there a women's Bible study at your local church you could join, if you aren't a part of one already, or a few friends you could invite to read through or study a book of the Bible together? Take a few moments now to plan how you will continue to make a daily habit of meeting with God in His Word and in prayer. It has been an absolute joy to journey through Colossians together, friend.

With love, Courtney.

ATTRIBUTES AND CHARACTERISTICS OF GOD[7]

Attentive

Compassionate

Creator

Deity*

Deliverer

Eternal

Faithful

Generous

Glorious

Gracious*

Good

Holy

Immanent*

Immutable/Unchanging

Incomprehensible

Infinite

Jealous

Just

Loving

Merciful

Miraculous*

Omnipotent (All-powerful)

Omnipresent (All-present)

Omniscient (All-knowing)

Paternal*

Patient/Long-suffering

Protector*

Provider

Redeemer*

Refuge

Righteous

Self-existent

Self-sufficient

Sovereign

Transcendent

Triune*

Truthful

Wise

Worthy

Wrathful

BIBLE STUDY TIPS

1. Read a shorter book in one sitting and in context of the greater story.

From Genesis to Revelation, the Bible tells us about who God is and His beautiful, redemptive plan to benevolently reign over His people. Throughout the Bible, we also see the "big story" of Scripture patterned that would include creation, fall, redemption, and restoration. God weaves the big story of the Bible in every single one of these sixty-six books that make up the Old and New Testaments. In God's creativity, these sixty-six books were written under the inspiration of the Holy Spirit and were written in different genre types: historical narrative, poetry, wisdom literature, law, prophecy, parables, epistles, and so on.

As we saw in the introductory material of this devotional guide, the book of Colossians falls under the genre of an epistle (a letter). So, if you think about receiving a letter yourself, how would you read it? Would you skip to the end and read the last few sentences? Would you start reading it and then stop after a few sentences? Would you skip around reading a little bit here, a little bit there? Of course not! You would sit down to read that letter from your loved one, and you'd read it start to finish.

So it makes sense that we should read these biblical letters in a similar way to keep the big picture and overall flow of the letter in mind as we read and study it. So, from time to time, it's good to read these shorter books of the Bible that are written as letters in one sitting. It helps us to read these books in the way they were intended to be read. It helps us to keep the book of the Bible in context. This will help you not only in Colossians but in any letter found in Scripture.

2. Read multiple translations.

Another wonderful tip as you dive deeper into Scripture is to read a passage in multiple translations. Some translations are "word for word"—their goal is to be as accurate as possible to the original language. Sometimes this means the reading will feel choppier, as the original language organizes sentences differently from the patterns English-speaking people use. But the payoff is accuracy. Other translations aim to translate in a "thought for thought" way—their goal is make sure the overall meaning of a passage is conveyed to a newcomer. Regardless of what passage you are studying, it helps to look up many translations to get an overall impression.

3. Repeat your reading.

Reading the same passage (or book) over and over again does something helpful: it builds our comprehension of the Scripture we are reading and our familiarity with it.

If you think about it, usually when you read something once, you aren't going to catch everything the writer is trying to say. You are naturally looking for the gist of the whole. To get the bits and details you missed, you have to go back and reread. This is true for all sorts of reading, and it's true of the Bible.

And here's a bonus: repeated reading also helps you memorize Scripture. I have never been great at Scripture memorization, but in my repeated reading I have been able to recall and locate passages or verses that come to mind faster. I now know their general location and context through the repeated reading I have done. It's sort of like watching a movie a few times. You know the key lines and the context in which those lines arise—all without even trying, simply because you happened to see the movie more than once. The fruit of repeated reading has been such a sweet gift from God to see how He is maturing me, so a few times throughout this devotional, you'll notice I've encouraged you to do the same.

4. Annotate.

Annotating means marking up the Scripture you're reading or studying. If you've never annotated before, here is a short list of a few ways you could try annotating:

> • Use colored pens or pencils. Mark words, phrases, or ideas you notice are repeated throughout the book you're reading. For example, the supremacy of Christ, how He is highest and best, is a central theme throughout the book of Colossians. Your type of annotating can be whatever makes most sense or comes most naturally to you, whether that's circling, underlining, using a symbol/icon, or something else. Annotating

doesn't have to be done one specific way, so there is freedom to try and explore annotating until you find what works best for you, friend!

- Put a question mark next to anything you read that you have a question about or may be confusing. Come back to it and write in your answer underneath it if that question gets answered along the way.
- Do you notice an attribute of God illustrated or celebrated as you read? Make note of that attribute as you read. Perhaps underline it in a designated color, or star it out on the margin.
- Are there transition words throughout the Scripture you're reading such as *therefore, if/then, likewise, because,* or *in the same way?* In the book of Colossians, we have seen both therefore and if/then transitions throughout the letter, so when you see these transition words come up, draw an arrow to connect the beginning argument and concluding thoughts the author wants you to notice.

5. Define new words.

Sometimes when you look at a passage, you see unfamiliar words. One great Bible study tip is to pause your reading when you come across a term you don't recognize, and look it up. This will add more context to what you're reading and help you gain a richer understanding of what the verse is saying. We tend to do this a lot when reading books outside of the Bible, like our favorite fiction book. But for some reason, we forget to do this when we read the Bible. Defining terms is helpful no matter what book you're reading, but it's all the more helpful when studying your Bible! For example, when I first read Colossians, I looked up words like *deity* and *elemental*. People don't use those terms in everyday language, after all. So when you come across a word or phrase you don't understand, don't feel embarrassed. Just look it up!

Another great tool to help you define words in the Bible is to look up the word used in the original language—either Hebrew or Greek, depending on which Testament you're in. I enjoy using the BlueLetterBible.org website to help me with this when I have more time to dig into the meaning of the original word.

6. Consider Bible study as a savings account rather than a debit account.

Finally, and probably the most important of these Bible study tips that has transformed the way I approach my own study of Scripture is remembering to approach Bible reading with patience. Jen Wilkin, in her book *Women of the Word*, opened my eyes to this patient approach in studying and reading the Bible. I want to pass it along to you:

> For years I viewed my interaction with the Bible
> as a debit account: I had a need, so I went to the
> Bible to withdraw an answer. But we do much
> better to view our interaction with the Bible as

a savings account: I stretch my understanding daily, I deposit what I glean, and I patiently wait for it to accumulate in value, knowing that one day I will need to draw on it. Bible study is an investment with a long-term payoff.[8]

We may not see the immediate, short-term benefits from our Bible reading and studying all the time. This is freeing in a sense; it means that if you don't have an amazing epiphany, a revolutionary "nugget" at the end of your time, or a powerful cry session with God as you read the Bible, that's okay! You are still doing exactly what you should be doing, and the Word of God is still hiding itself in your heart. Keep depositing the Word in your heart, day by day, paragraph by paragraph, chapter by chapter, book by book. It *will* produce fruit in due season! As you read another book of the Bible months from now, or years from now, you'll make connections you wouldn't have seen without faithful patience through past books of the Bible that you've studied.

Keep making those daily deposits, friend!

NOTES

1. Dane Ortlund, *Gentle and Lowly: The Heart of Christ for Sinners and Sufferers* (Wheaton, IL: Crossway, 2020), 89.

2. Eugene Peterson paraphrases Colossians 2:6–7 this way in *The Message Bible*.

3. C. S. Lewis, *Complete Works of C. S. Lewis* (Kyiv, Ukraine: Strelbytskyy Multimedia Publishing, 2021), accessed May 19, 2022, https://www.google.com/books/edition/Complete_Works_of_C_S_Lewis_Illustrated/31DuDwAAQBAJ?hl=en&gbpv=1&dq=%22I+found+that+all+the+pain+had+gone+from+my+arm.+And+then+I+saw+why.+I%27d+turned+into+a+boy+again%22&pg=PT315&printsec=frontcover.

4. Richard R. Melick Jr., *New American Commentary: Philippians, Colossians, Philemon* (Nashville: B&H Publishing, 1991), 312.

5. Melick Jr., *New American Commentary: Philippians, Colossians, Philemon*, 315.

6. "Preface to the English Standard Version," ESV Study Bible, accessed May 21, 2022, https://www.esv.org/preface.

7. This list was adapted with a few additions from Jen Wilkin's study of the book of Exodus: *God of Deliverance: A Study of Exodus 1–18* (Nashville: Lifeway Press, 2021), 172–73. The attributes with an astrict were added by the author as an addition to Jen's list.

8. Jen Wilkin, *Women of the Word: How to Study the Bible with Both Our Hearts and Our Minds* (Wheaton, IL: Crossway, 2014), 81.

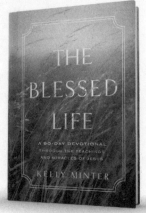